DRAW!

A Visual Approach to Thinking, Learning and Communicating

Kurt Hanks and Larry Belliston

WILLIAM KAUFMANN, INC.
One First Street
Los Altos, California 94022

Many people and organizations have been
immensely helpful in the preparation of this
book. Their gracious and unselfish
contributions are tremendously appreciated.
Thanks to each and all.

This book was designed by:

Information Design

444 South 6th East
Salt Lake City, Utah   84102

Library of Congress Cataloging in Publication Data

Hanks, Kurt, 1947-
    Draw.

    Bibliography: p.
    Includes index.
    1. Drawing Psychology of. 2. Thought and thinking.
3. Learning Psychology of. 4. Interpersonal communication.
I. Belliston, Larry, 1946-
II. Title.
BF456.D7H27   152.3'845   77-6328
ISBN 0-913232-45-9

Contents

Re-establish drawing in your life. We all have an innate drawing ability and desire. Children do it for fun. Adults often doodle to relax and pass the time. Everyone can add the dimension of drawing for a purpose.

Drawing is a means to an end—a tool to help solve problems, create new ideas and assist communication.

Learn how to draw more proficiently and enjoyably.

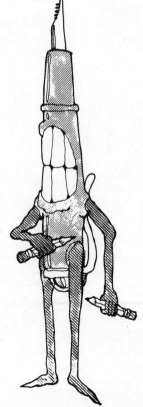

Rapid Visualization

Expanding the mind. Drawing to capture fleeting mental images. Drawing as an extension of the mind onto a piece of paper.

Ideation

Creating. Drawing as a reflection of the creative mind. Probing, testing, refining and developing our individual visions. Drawing and visualizing as new ways of looking at the same old world and creating a new one.

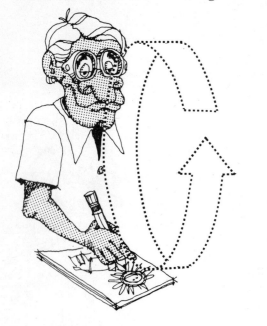

Notation

Learning and remembering. Drawing to help understand concepts and recall what we have learned. Getting information into our memory and back out again.

Communication

Drawing as a means of communicating a message from one person to another. "A picture is worth a thousand words." Drawing as a system of image transfer and storage.

Introduction

Whether or not you intend to become an illustrator, graphic designer, doodler, or any kind of artist for that matter, this book is designed to help you. What is it all about? It is partly about you—at least something that you can do. All of us as young children had our time at the table with a pack of crayolas and a piece of paper. In school or at home, drawing is something we all just naturally do. It is simply an activity that effectively expands the ideas, visions and dreams we see in our minds when we are young. A piece of paper with the wiggly lines and bright colors we made as children helped us learn about our world and some of the exciting things in it.

And people of all ages "doodle." We often make squiggles and other funny lines with a pen on paper as we talk on the phone or converse with friends. We relax in this way and feel comfortable doing it. Down inside, most of us like to draw even though we may not realize it or admit it.

But we sometimes fail to realize what drawing can do for us. We may not understand that drawing can again become a useful visual tool to help us with life's situations. Since we grew up, many of us have relegated drawing to a position of unimportance in our lives—something that we needn't waste our time on, or something that artists do for a living or to hang on museum walls.

Drawing, however, can be much more than that. It can be a source of great satisfaction, and it can help us in learning, thinking and communicating. Therefore, we ask you to

study this book carefully. It is not made to be set on an end table like one of those pretty picture books that people give each other as presents. It is designed to be used. This book should be questioned, modified, written in and drawn in (unless you have borrowed it or are using a library copy!).

The drawings in this book were chosen as examples to illustrate a point. Many of the drawings are of very good quality—fine illustrations done by top-notch professionals. If you are just beginning to draw and do not yet consider yourself a seasoned illustrator, don't be discouraged by the high quality drawings in this book. It is desirable to learn how to draw by studying from the best illustrators' work and techniques.

Drawing is a learned skill. Not everyone who draws will be an artist, some people seem to be born with a greater ability to draw. Desire and practice, however, often enable a less capable person to produce drawings far superior in quality than those of a lazy but gifted person.

You learn to walk by walking. You learn to talk by talking. You learn to read by reading. You learn to write by writing. And you learn to draw by drawing. Drawing is a learned skill.

You will be pleasantly surprised to see the gradual improvements in your own drawings and sketches as you study, learn and practice. Draw!

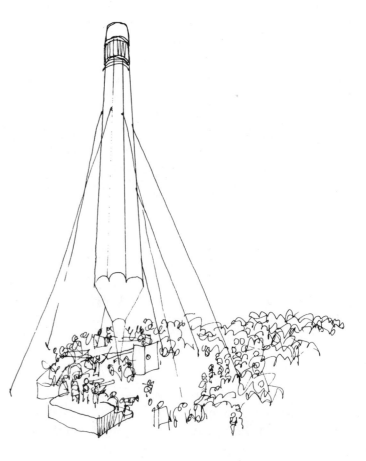

Da-Da-Ta-Da-Ta-Da!

And God said, let us
make man in our image
after our likeness . . .
Genesis 1:26

Anyone Can Draw

It is a child's natural way to use art as a personal language. The child invents new ways to tell us about his ideas, impressions and feelings. This natural approach results in the exciting designs which make children's art so vital ....

Victor D'Amico

With tongue cocked off to one side, nose positioned just inches from a piece of scratch paper and fingers locked tightly around a yellow pencil, a five-year-old's hand moves in short, jerky motions as he labors over a drawing. His face radiates with complete involvment in what he's doing. He is ecstatic with the opportunity to draw and communicate his ideas and knowledge.

Almost without exception, children love to draw. But what happens to most of them later in life? Drawing, for many, is relegated to a position of unimportance. Children draw to express their fantasies and dreams, what they have learned and what they can accomplish; all much unlike the reserved non-drawing grown-ups we become. Drawing is a joyous experience of communication and expression for children—and it can be a similar positive experience for us as we grow older.

1

You're not an artist!

You can't draw!

That is ugly!

**Ha! Ha!
Ha! Ha! Ha! Ha!
Ha! Ha! Ha!
Ha! Ha!**

**Criticism destroys
more drawings than
any other thing**

Dr. Seuss, the famous writer and illustrator of children's books was once asked why he would draw so funny. "It's because I can't draw," he replied. "I just do the natural thing to do, and I can't draw any other way."

His supposed lack of drawing ability was fortunate for him—it made him a wealthy and famous individual.

**Dr. Seuss
was asked
"why do you
draw so
strangely?"**

**"That's the
only way I
can draw."**

What is drawing? Almost everyone describes it as something an artist mysteriously produces on canvas. And drawing is all too often associated with a work of art like the Mona Lisa or some other masterpiece. But to a child, drawing is an exciting personal medium. Ask a child to draw and he will bubble with excitement. Ask an adult to draw and he will give you a myriad of excuses—he says, in essence, he doesn't think he can produce a masterpiece. He's afraid to try.

Criticism, prejudice, ridicule and insecurity stifle most people's desire and willingness to draw. After all, if we cannot produce a masterpiece we must not be any good, so why try?

But is that what drawing is all about? Can there be anything more to it?

What is drawing?

draw·ing \ˈdroi-)iŋ\ *n* **1** : an act or instance of drawing; *specif* : the process of deciding something by drawing lots **2** : the art or technique of representing an object or outlining a figure, plan, or sketch by means of lines **3** : something drawn or subject to drawing: as **a** : an amount drawn from a fund **b** : a representation formed by drawing : SKETCH

This book discusses drawing in a much different manner than the usual text of drawing. It adds the dimension of drawing for a purpose. It treats drawing as a means of more effective communication, understanding, expression and enjoyment. The way of drawing explained in this book is more closely related to quick sketches drawn on scratch paper at lunch as a point is explained to a friend than to the Mona Lisa. Drawing becomes the tool rather than the finished work.

Drawing can be a medium which brings problems into visual form where they can be evaluated, refined, understood, communicated and resolved. Drawing in this definition is a process—not an end in itself.

The book teaches drawing as a tool we can all use. It takes drawing out of the "mysterious thing that only an artist does" stage and builds it into a talent we all possess and can use constructively.

"No longer can we consider the artistic process as self contained, mysteriously inspired from above, unrelated and unrelatable to what people do otherwise."

Rudolph Arnheim

David, age 5

3

Drawing Is A Tool

Drawing is a means to an end, a tool to help solve problems, create new ideas and assist communication.

The underlying principle of this book is that drawing should not always be considered the end result, but that it is often a means to an end. Drawing is not only a piece of "art work" but is often a help to understanding, communication, ideation, and problem solving.

Most people probably lack the coordination, temperament, desire or skill to become a fine artist—a producer of masterpieces or show art. But most people can use drawing to good advantage. Even the fine artist could put drawing to work for him by using it as a means to an end.

To race car drivers, auto mechanics, or new car dealers, the automobile may be an end in itself. But for most of us, the automobile is simply a modern convenience which makes transportation from one place to another faster and easier. Cars help us get to work and do our traveling more efficiently. For most of us,

Drawing is a process, not a product

Draw, Doodle, Sketch!

5

cars are not our work. And the same is true of drawing. Drawing may never provide the primary source of livelihood, but it can be a useful means to an end. Many professionals who are not artists—architects, engineers, inventors, mathematicians, geologists, physicians, sociologists, and others—can think and communicate more effectively through the use of drawing and visualization.

Think of something, anything—a store grocery list, an incident that happened to you, an old friend, something that needs to be done—anything. As you thought, you probably had a visual image come to mind. You "saw" in your mind's eye whatever you related to your thought. It is this mental visualizing we all do that this book builds upon. Enhance your natural thought processes by expanding upon a mainstay of mental thought—visualization. This book is designed to show you how.

TO DRAW IS TO SEE

Visualization is a method of expressing and evaluating what our mind conceives. Visualization, when working effectively, is a cycle in which a drawing is done to allow testing and evaluation of a visual concept, as the following diagram shows:

Express Test Cycle

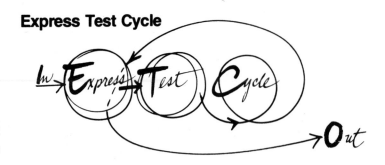

Experiences in Visual Thinking, Robert McKim, Brooks/Cole Publishing Co.

One purpose of the visualization method of drawing for our mind expansion is to capture the mind's images for further evaluation. The method used to make visualization work more effectively is illustrated above as an Express-Test-Cycle Method. It means to draw what you think (drawing includes written words at times) and then evaluate what you have drawn.

It is a natural process for our minds to quickly evaluate our thoughts and ideas. The mind often passes judgment on our mental images without considering the details. Thoughts come and go so quickly that we pass over many important points. The mind passes judgment (yes-no, good-bad, like-dislike) too hastily sometimes. However, for many important issues, the judgment should be deferred until after a drawing is made and pertinent details become more and more obvious as the drawing progresses.

One of the many things that drawing does is create the need to study and answer details. Drawing stimulates imagination and thinking.

Drawing includes the ability to see what is to be drawn, as well as the ability to transfer that image onto a surface.

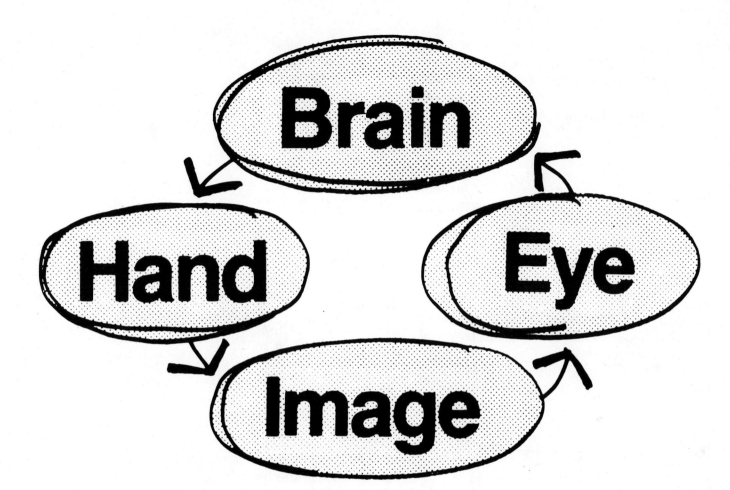

**Drawing is a cycle—a continual
process of development and expression.**

As a process of thinking or understanding,
drawing begins with the hand expressing a
visual image and the trained eye and mind
evaluating and changing the drawing as it
develops. Drawing can be considered a
complete process . . . a cycle.

Drawing can be a representation of what we
see or what we think or want to see. It can be
a representation of reality or an abstract idea
made manifest in a real form. We abstract what
we see to create a drawing. We transform
abstract thoughts and ideas into reality
through drawing.

This page shows how drawings can help evolve ideas. Drawing here includes sketching and using the language of verbal notation and perspective to probe thinking from varied viewpoints and levels of abstraction.

Louis Kahn, a well-known architect, looked at his creations as they evolved from an abstract to a finished form through the medium of visual sketches. Drawing helped him to think.

This sketch is taken from Thomas A. Edison's personal notebook.

Edison used drawings to help him create and better understand his many inventions, in this case, the electric light bulb.

For Edison and Kahn, drawing provided a valuable medium for inventing and testing ideas. Drawing was actually a part of their inventive process.

The Development by Louis Kahn of the Design for the Second Capitol of Pakistan, Dacca,
© Student Publications, School of Design, North Carolina State University.

The refinement of ideas on a much larger scale is made possible through the medium of quick sketches. This drawing is an example of the architect's idea of future buildings.

A. Quincy Jones/Architect, A. Quincy Jones and Associates, Architects, Inc., Los Angeles

9

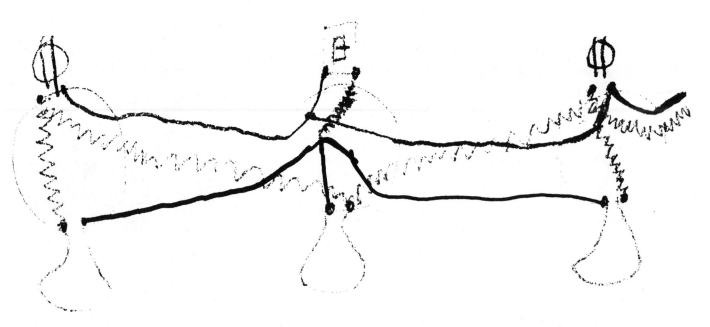

The drawing below is a reproduction of a label attached to the United States satellite Pioneer 10 which traveled beyond our solar system. The label is being used in an attempt to communicate, through visual images, with other intelligences that may exist in the universe.

The above illustration was also used to aid thinking and understanding. It is a rapid sketch made to help someone put wiring in one room of his house correctly.

These drawings show different styles, but each was used as a tool to accomplish the aims of its particular situation.

Kids do it!

David, age 5

Visualization is a method of easy communication, as well as of advanced thinking and understanding.

NASA

Studies of the works of the Italian artist and inventor Leonardo da Vinci (1452-1519) have indicated that he was probably of only average intelligence. But by being able to think visually Leonardo da Vinci accomplished much more in his lifetime than others of his same capabilities were able to do. He became an engineer, an inventor, a physiologist and generally an astute thinker. The drawings indicate some of the visual ideations and solutions to problems that he understood and communicated.

Many of his inventions were years ahead of his time. Scholars believe, for example, that Leonardo conceived the bicycle chain drive hundreds of years before it became reality. Actual application of the drive did not come until the 19th century.

Drawing is a direct means for understanding reality.

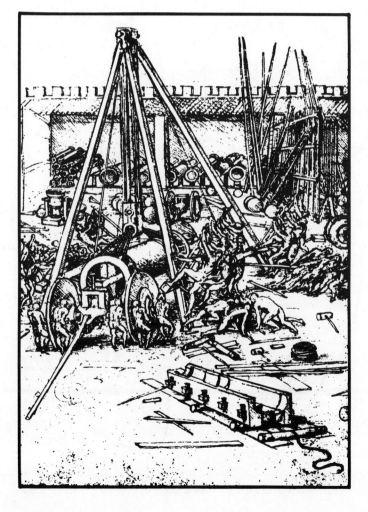

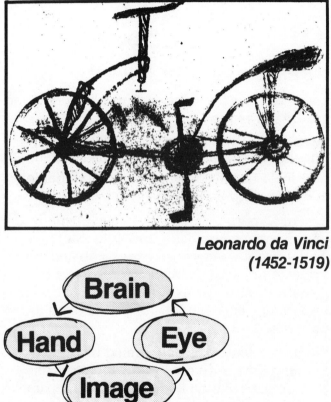

Leonardo da Vinci
(1452-1519)

All drawing whether the efforts of a five-year-old or the sketches of Leonardo da Vinci, give visual form to thoughts. Drawing is an evolutionary cycle involving our brains, our eyes, our hands and our interpretations of visual images.

11

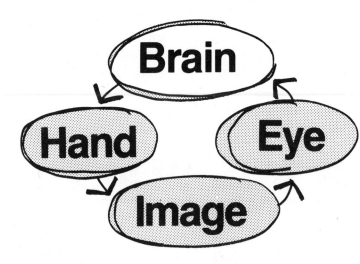

The Brain

Let's consider the relationship of the brain and mind to drawing.

Drawing is a projection of the mind on paper. It is a mental activity before it becomes a physical one. All drawing is a representation of mental impressions.

Recent scientific discoveries have dramatized the importance of visualization to thinking. And since drawing is an expression and extension of visualization, a knowledge of visualization helps us better understand the importance and relationship of the brain to drawing.

Medical science has determined that the human brain is divided into two halves or hemispheres. These hemispheres are separated by a "corpus callosum" (a bundle of interconnecting fibers). The left side of the body is mainly controlled by the right hemisphere of the brain and the right side of the body is controlled by the left hemisphere. When we talk of using the left hand, we mean the left hand being controlled by the right side of the brain and vice versa.

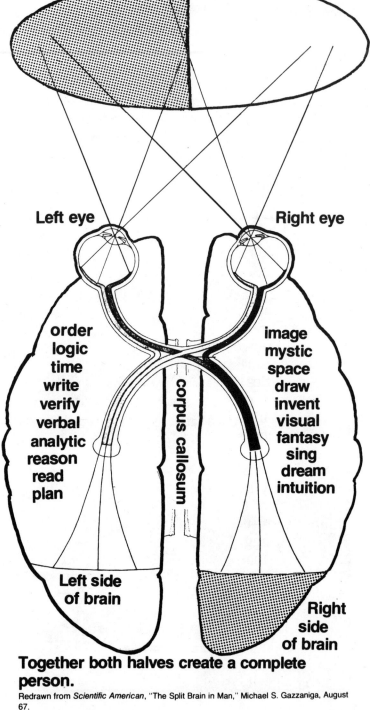

Left eye   Right eye

order
logic
time
write
verify
verbal
analytic
reason
read
plan

corpus callosum

image
mystic
space
draw
invent
visual
fantasy
sing
dream
intuition

Left side of brain

Right side of brain

Together both halves create a complete person.

Redrawn from *Scientific American*, "The Split Brain in Man," Michael S. Gazzaniga, August 67.

Medical science has discovered that the two hemispheres of the brain also "think" differently. For most normal people the left hemisphere of the brain thinks analytically, logically and verbally. The right side, however, thinks in a more artistic sense. The right hemisphere is primarily responsible for visual thinking– recognition of faces and objects, crafts, orientation in space, artistic endeavor.

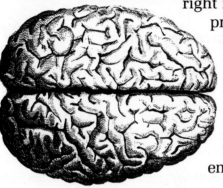

The fact that everyone has two "brains" which think differently is reason enough to activate the brain power of *both* hemispheres. Much of our education is centered around the language and analytical skills. This sharpens one hemisphere of the brain—the left hemisphere. However, in many people the visual thinking (or right hemisphere) of the brain is not developed to a very high potential. It is the belief of the authors that visual development also greatly increases mental ability. It enables better use of the visual half the brain which is often needlessly at rest and is under-utilized. (See the Suggested Readings pages 238-239 for more information on this complex subject.) The significance of this knowledge, at least from the authors' point of view, is that our minds ought to be exercised in the visual thinking area through such activities as drawing and imagining. A normal person who uses both hemispheres to full potential may accomplish more mentally than someone who does not.

Drawing is partly a mental activity, not simply a physical one.

Project your mind onto the paper

13

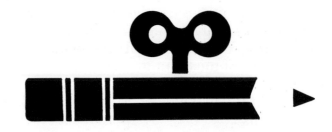

Idea sketches

A pencil is a tool run by a mind

C. Joshua Abend, Vice president, Industrial Design, SCM Corp.

Shown here are the idea sketches used to solve some of the questions surrounding distress flares. Each sketch brought new considerations, new problems or new solutions. Using sketches to thoroughly

evaluate the new invention helped evolve a better flare.

Some of the world's greatest people have used the visual side of the brain to tremendously help them.

Albert Einstein used visualization as well as analytical thinking to enable him to formulate and more fully understand his time and energy theories. He termed using *both* sides of his brain or consciousness as "combinatory play" and claimed that it was important for creativity. An example of how visualization helped him understand motion and energy is demonstrated in the following anecdote. He tells of picturing a man holding a sphere in his arms and standing in a cage which is being pulled away from the earth by a long rope. He asks the question: If the man lets go of the sphere does it fall to the floor of the cage, as we think gravity causes things to do, or does the cage move up to meet the sphere? The formulation of the energy-motion problem and its solution both depended heavily upon Einstein's ability to visualize as well as analyze.

But not only artists like Leonardo da Vinci or scientists like Albert Einstein have used drawing and visualization to greatly expand their minds.

14

For example, sports figures also use visualization and drawing. Diagrams of plays help teams function better, and meditation ("visual exercising") helps individuals perform better. Johnny Miller, one of golf's first million-dollar winners, claimed that he improved his golf swing by picturing it in his mind.

Can you think of other examples of people who have improved their creativity and accomplishments by learning to visualize and draw?

"If you would learn to draw, hold the instrument often and hold it with your head."

William Kirby Lockard

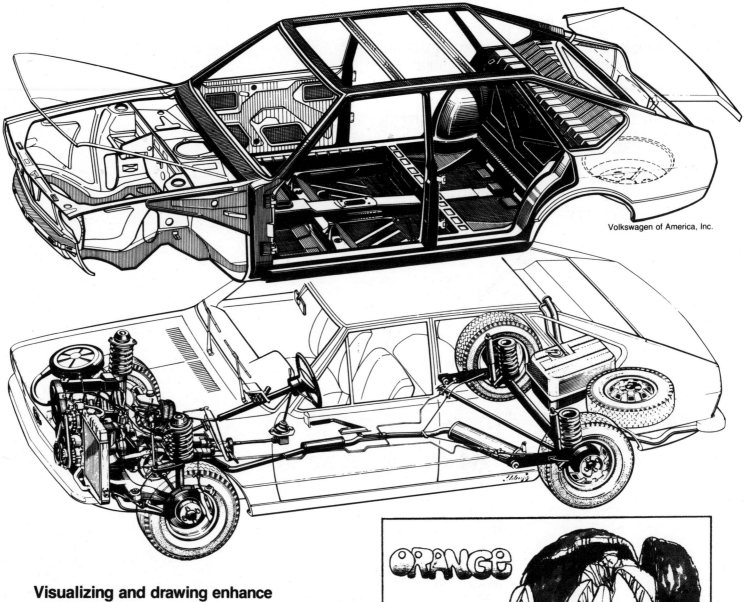

Volkswagen of America, Inc.

Visualizing and drawing enhance understanding. . . .

Drawing enables us to understand the structure, parts and relationship of the parts of an object. By making detailed drawings of a car or an orange, we are quickly able to understand how it is put together, what its parts are, and how different areas relate.

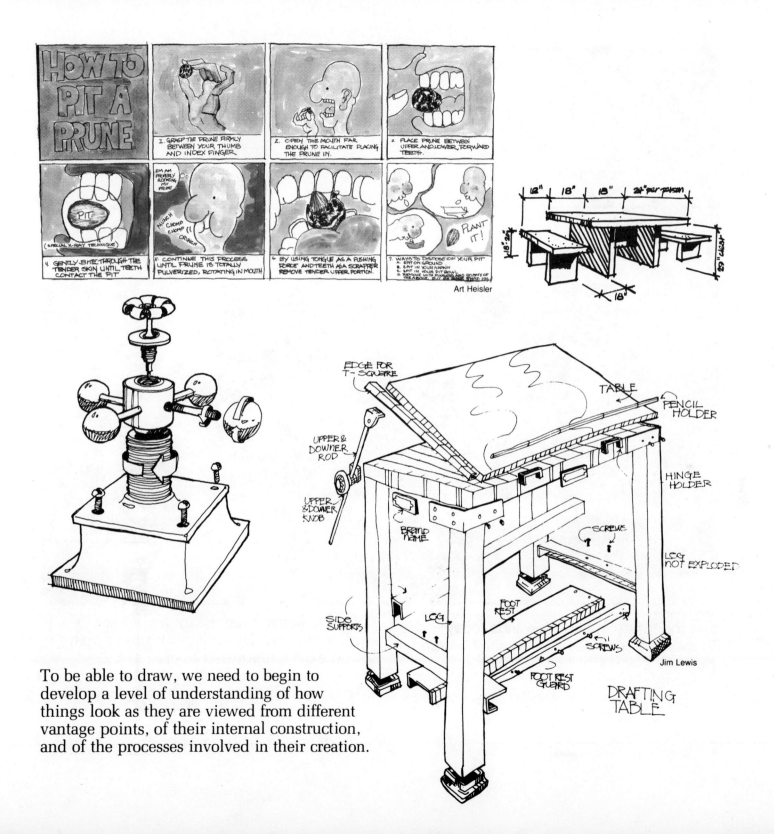

To be able to draw, we need to begin to develop a level of understanding of how things look as they are viewed from different vantage points, of their internal construction, and of the processes involved in their creation.

17

FIELD NEXT 15
ROMA 100 AD. EMP. TRAJAN. FO

**See the future in your drawings today
to evaluate your ideas before they become
reality.**

Drawing helps bring the future into the
reality of today. It provides visions of what
could exist tomorrow but is just being
designed, developed and evaluated today.
Sketching helps to see ideas while they are
still being formulated—while they are still
subject to improvement, rather than after they
are solidified in a physical form.

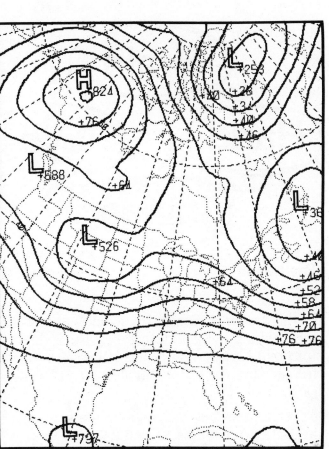

Drawing is the beginning of an idea.

All these drawings were the visualizations of future ideas, of things that did not exist when the drawings were first made. The building had yet to be built, but in the architect's mind it already existed as a building that could be lived in. The weather map is an image of how the weatherman sees tomorrow's weather today. The camera's first "pictures" exist only in the designer's imagination.

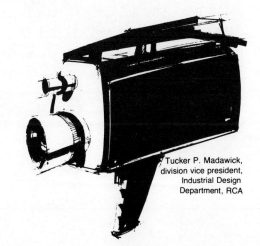

Tucker P. Madawick, division vice president, Industrial Design Department, RCA

19

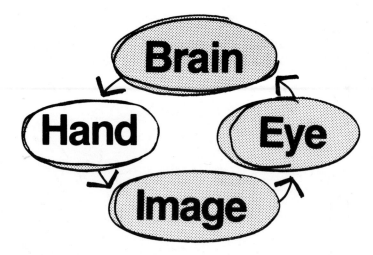

The Hand

Drawing and understanding go hand in hand.

In the drawing process the hand is one of the tools which helps to transform visual ideas into reality or to clarify visual images by transferring them from an abstract to a real form.

Man as an animal is unique in many ways, including his hands, which function very effectively. Our hands, which give us the ability to use drawing implements and other tools, open possibilities to us that are not available to other animals. Some other animals may have the ability to visualize images, but man is the only creature able to change those visual images into a sort of instant reality by drawing pictures of them for others to share.

Being able to communicate in this way, man can refine his thoughts and ideas by interacting with others before transforming these ideas into real objects—from day-to-day consumer products to whole cities.

Drawing gives us many advantages. If we draw in the notes we make to ourselves, we are often better able to recall and remember.

Drawing can be much quicker than writing. Communicating to someone how to get to a certain place can be very difficult if done in writing. Draw a simple map and see how much easier the task becomes.

Drawing is an aid to understanding. As something is drawn it becomes more concrete and clear to the mind.

The human hand, composed of the fingers and an opposing thumb, makes man unique in his ability to use tools—including those for drawing.

This is a page taken from the diary record of the Lewis and Clark expedition (1804). Drawings formed a good portion of their record. Instead of writing in words they wrote using a combination of pictures and words. Their diary is both interesting and understandable.

Oh magic hands, guide this pencil along the way to paths I've never traveled and into visions I've never seen.
Harry Hanns

William Blake (1757-1827) English poet, artist and engraver communicated a provoking thought when he wrote—
"To see a World in a Grain of Sand
And a Heaven in a Wild Flower,
Hold Infinity in the palm of your hand
And Eternity in an hour."

Most people become so proficient at writing that they can write almost without thinking about it. In the beginning, writing each letter is a laborious process. As we become more familiar with our language writing becomes almost a subconscious skill.

Drawing can become just as familiar. We can learn to draw almost automatically and no matter how primitive our drawings are they won't be worse than the handwriting of others.

If you are unaccustomed to drawing, it may seem difficult at first. But with practice and time it will become easier. As drawing proficiency increases so will your enjoyment and your benefit from drawing.

In the beginning, forget about how good or how poor your drawings are. Don't judge the quality of those drawings—just draw.

Kirk Henrichsen

The more you practice the better you become.

22

Each drawing teaches new insights which can be applied to present or future problems. These insights can be continually reapplied to the process.

This drawing shows a combination of visual and verbal terms.

Your hand will develop in skill in direct proportion to how your mind uses it and to how often you draw.

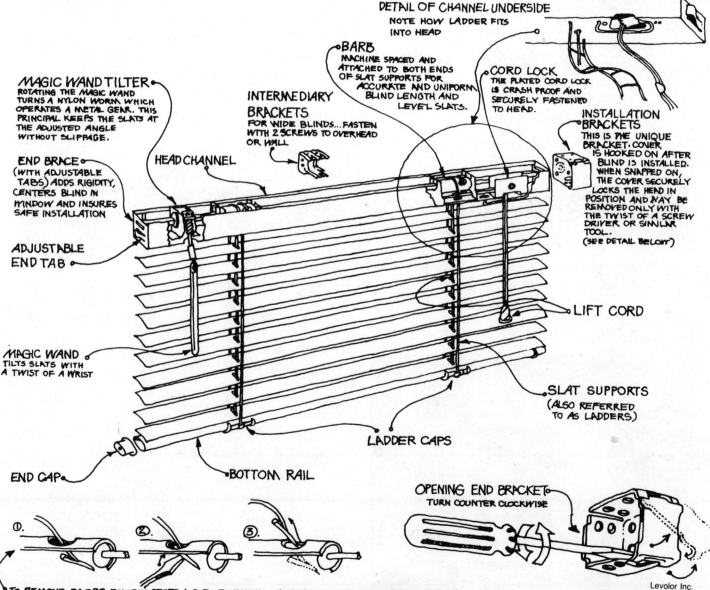

DETAIL OF CHANNEL UNDERSIDE
NOTE HOW LADDER FITS INTO HEAD

BARB
MACHINE SPACED AND ATTACHED TO BOTH ENDS OF SLAT SUPPORTS FOR ACCURATE AND UNIFORM BLIND LENGTH AND LEVEL SLATS.

CORD LOCK
THE PLATED CORD LOCK IS CRASH PROOF AND SECURELY FASTENED TO HEAD.

INSTALLATION BRACKETS
THIS IS THE UNIQUE BRACKET. COVER IS HOOKED ON AFTER BLIND IS INSTALLED. WHEN SNAPPED ON, THE COVER SECURELY LOCKS THE HEAD IN POSITION AND MAY BE REMOVED ONLY WITH THE TWIST OF A SCREW DRIVER OR SIMILAR TOOL. (SEE DETAIL BELOW)

MAGIC WAND TILTER
ROTATING THE MAGIC WAND TURNS A NYLON WORM WHICH OPERATES A METAL GEAR. THIS PRINCIPAL KEEPS THE SLATS AT THE ADJUSTED ANGLE WITHOUT SLIPPAGE.

INTERMEDIARY BRACKETS
FOR WIDE BLINDS...FASTEN WITH 2 SCREWS TO OVERHEAD OR WALL

END BRACE
(WITH ADJUSTABLE TABS) ADDS RIGIDITY, CENTERS BLIND IN WINDOW AND INSURES SAFE INSTALLATION

HEAD CHANNEL

ADJUSTABLE END TAB

LIFT CORD

MAGIC WAND
TILTS SLATS WITH A TWIST OF A WRIST

SLAT SUPPORTS
(ALSO REFERRED TO AS LADDERS)

LADDER CAPS

END CAP

BOTTOM RAIL

OPENING END BRACKET
TURN COUNTER CLOCKWISE

①. ②. ③.

TO REMOVE BARBS FOLLOW STEPS 1,2,3. TO INSTALL BARBS FOLLOW STEPS IN REVERSE 3,2,1.

Levolor Inc.

23

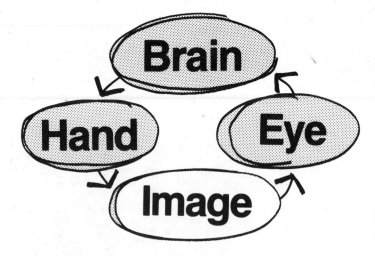

That which we see creates some sort of image in our mind. Many things are obvious and we see them so often that their images pass by apparently without registering. Think of a telephone dial for instance. You have seen it hundreds of times and it is fairly simple. Yet could you describe it in detail, placing the numbers and the corresponding letters of the alphabet correctly together around the circular dial? Most people can't.

In contrast, the symbols below have very significant and profound meanings for most of us. Not only do we see the symbols, but their meanings, quite often, bring to mind additional images, emotions and reactions.

The Image

The third part of the drawing process is IMAGE. Image refers to what you think you see as opposed to what you actually see.

Most of us are familiar with the visual illusion illustrated below. As you look at the positive shape (the white area) you see the image of a vase. Now look again at the dark area and you see two silhouettes looking at each other. First you saw a vase, the next time two faces—two completely unrelated images from the same illustration.

Images are a good reminder that people can learn to see more than they do. Each person sees what he is trained to see.

Scribble a line—make something from it

When you were younger you probably played a game similar to the one on the next page. Given a line in a square, make something from what you see. Complete the drawing. Try this with someone else and you will find that most everyone sees a completely different image for each square. Try it!

24

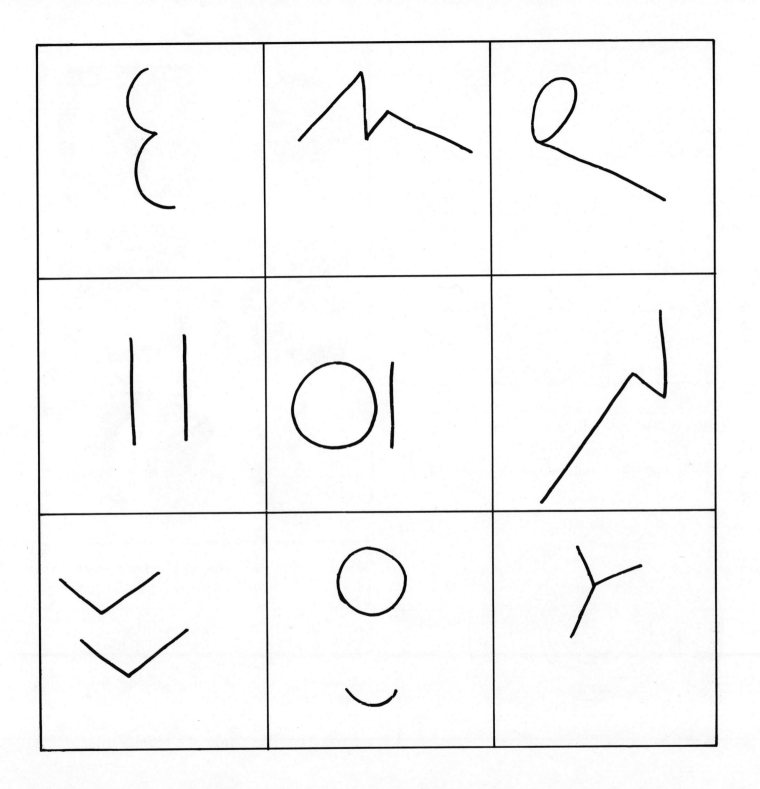

These are the finished images of what one person saw in the lines on the previous page. Did you see the same thing?

The concentric circles show the solar system as Copernicus imagined it.

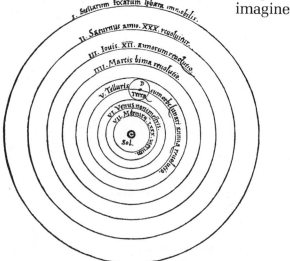

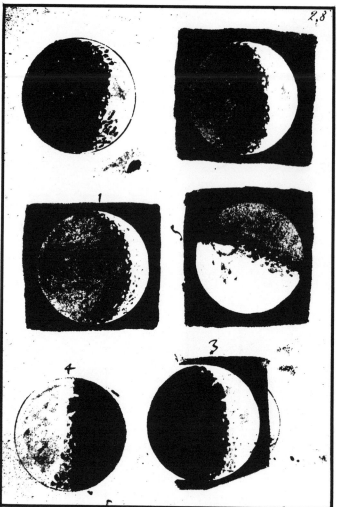

The drawings of the moon were done by Galileo. He recorded his work by drawing what he saw.

Copernicus (1473-1543) and Galileo (1564-1642) saw the world from a different point of view. Their image of the world beyond this earth was quite different from that of their fellow men.

Many different images are derived from what we see. The illustration of a termite colony

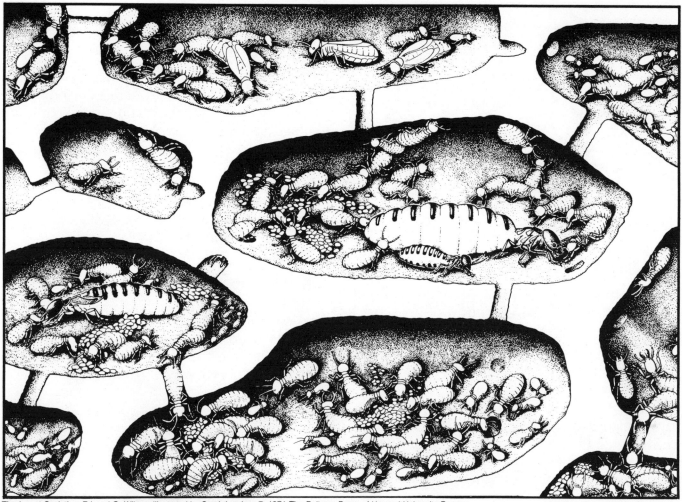

The Insect Societies, Edward O. Wilson, illustrated by Sarah Landry, © 1971 The Belknap Press of Harvard University Press.

may communicate social structure, living environment or method of destruction employed by this household pest.

The architectural rendering may remind us of a home we've seen, a cabin away from the city or just a nice place to be.

Or we might combine the pictures in our mind and conclude that termites have invaded the beautiful structure.

What you see is what you get.

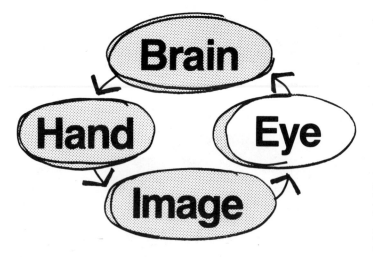

The Eye

The eye plays a significant part in most of our lives. A study by the Department of the Navy concluded that 95 percent of all information is received through our eyes. Have you ever heard the term "seeing is believing?" Well, you can believe it.

If visual input is such a significant part of our lives, then it would logically follow that drawing could also have a profound influence on our lives. Drawing helps us to learn to see more accurately and in greater depth.

To be able to draw you must interpret what you see accurately. One of the first rules of drawing is to draw what you actually see. When ten different people draw the same thing you would expect that each of the drawings would be slightly different—size, emphasis, medium used—but often ten people will actually "see" ten different things in one object.

To draw well you must begin by drawing what is really there. See reality, not what you think about, what you see or what your mind may fail to comprehend. Many artists take license with reality, but they begin by drawing reality so that "distortion," such as surrealism, can take proper dimension later on.

Try this mental exercise to enhance your seeing accuracy. Think of yourself walking up to a solid black curtain. You can't see beyond the curtain except that you notice two small holes cut just so that you can look through with both eyes. Notice how the world beyond the black shield takes on an interesting and magnificent depth. Study what you see. Notice the brilliance and intricacy.

"Oh, say, can you see?"

That's what it's all about. Look at the world as though it were a treat, a unique opportunity. Study what you see as though you were going to draw it, and your eyes will see more than they ever have before.

What do you see? Look beyond what is apparent, and remember . . .

The great virtue of vision is that it is not only a highly articulate medium, but that its universe offers inexhaustibly rich information about the objects and events of the outer world. Therefore, vision is the primary medium of thought.

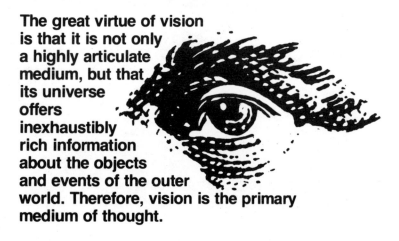

Rudolf Arnheim

Drawing . . . "has nothing to do with artifice or technique. It has nothing to do with aesthetics or conception. It has only to do with the act of correct observation, and by that I mean a physical contact with all sorts of objects through all the senses."
                    Kimon Nicolaides

Some people cannot draw because they do not take the time and effort to see accurately. As they begin to see accurately and in detail their drawing ability increases.

Drawing—a way of seeing the world

Drawing allows us to see the unseeable
and picture how it works. Whether it be
unseeable history (above) or the physicist's
concept of nuclear fission (below), drawing
allows us to see what words cannot adequately
describe.

One picture is worth a thousand words. Old Chinese Saying

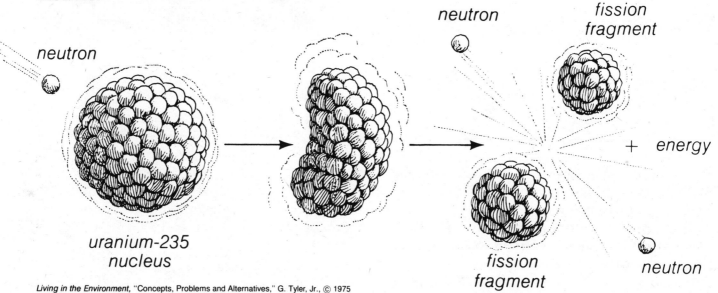

neutron

*uranium-235
nucleus*

neutron

*fission
fragment*

+ *energy*

*fission
fragment*

neutron

30

Living in the Environment, "Concepts, Problems and Alternatives," G. Tyler, Jr., © 1975
Wadsworth Publishing Co.

Isadora and Her Avocado Plant.©

Oh! The End is near.

Goodbye cruel world.

There really IS life after salad!

Drawing allows us to see a salad from an avocado's point of view, or a kitchen in different light.

Drawing actually helps us to expand our minds. It allows us to see the past or the future.

How else can drawing help open our eyes? Try it and find out. There really is a world worth looking closely at!

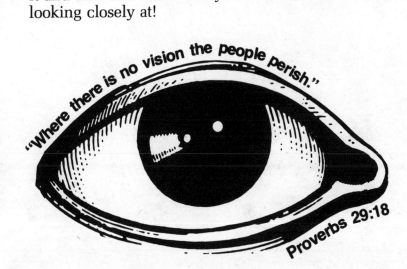

"Where there is no vision the people perish."

Proverbs 29:18

31

Methods, Tools and Techniques

The seed lies in the verb to draw. To draw requires an action, a performance, and this—the act of drawing.
Edward Hill

A working knowledge of the various drawing tools, methods and techniques enables us to draw better. Just like any other skill, an understanding of the variables which govern performance enables us to be better at that skill. Drawing is no different.

As you study the next pages, please remember that they are just suggestions. Not every method or tool or every technique will apply to all situations. Pick and choose, use only what applies. If you can find a better way, use it!

Cook up a drawing

Drawing is somewhat like cooking. With any recipe a number of cooks would produce results that taste slightly different. The end result depends on how carefully the cook mixes the ingredients and in what order. The end result also depends upon how and with what method the things are cooked. Charcoal broiling makes food taste different than does frying or baking, for example.

The finished drawing, like the finished meal, depends upon the tools used (the ingredients), how well they are used and in what manner (the recipe) and the technique or style employed (the cooking medium). Often, it doesn't really matter how the different things are varied because many variations can produce quality results. A broader knowledge of the possibilities does enable better or easier results, however. Once again, use what you need or like to fit your circumstance or purpose.

The analogy to drawing might be:

Finished food = Finished drawing
Recipe = Method
Ingredients = Tools
Cooking Medium = Technique

B.C. by permission of Johnny Hart and Field Enterprises, Inc.

Every graphic expression embodies a viewpoint, a single way of looking at reality. Every time the thinker changes graphic languages he submits his ideas to a new set of built-in mental operations.

Robert McKim

Drawings can take on a different look about as easily as a change of clothes gives us a different look. By changing the drawing tools, the method or the technique, the appearance of a drawing changes drastically. The same drawing done in pen and ink looks quite different from one done in pastels. And one using ink and pen looks different from one using ink and brush. One using ink and pen done with contour lines is different from one with ink and pen in a cross hatch pattern.

Change your clothes and your drawing techniques depending on the situation.

"Before beginning to compose something, gauge the nature and extent of the enterprise and work for a suitable design. Design improves even the simplest structure whether of brick and steel or of prose. You raise a pup tent from one sort of vision, a cathedral from another."

E. B. White

The end result of a drawing, to a large degree, is determined by the tools and the technique used. Or, the tools and technique used, to a large degree, can be determined by the end result desired.

The importance of technique and tools cannot be overlooked. Each has its purpose and place. You would not use a hammer to tighten a bolt or a wrench to drive a nail. Likewise you would not use oils to make a rough sketch nor pencils to create finished art on most canvas. Learn to recognize and use different media, tools, and techniques if they can help you.

The First Pencil

Don't be afraid to try new things.

if you
can
find
a better
way

USE IT!

Tools

The tool is only as good as the person using it.

A considerable number of tools are available for the would-be artist. And, (fortunately for the industry) most artists are suckers to try them all. If a new Captain Whiz-bang pen with 39 colored cartridges becomes available, many people will buy it. But are all these things necessary?

If you are just beginning to draw, we suggest the initial use of simple pencils and pens. You will draw and feel most comfortable with pens and pencils to begin with. We prefer the use of pens for doodling and initial sketching. Pens are convenient and they create a free and fluid work. Since you cannot erase ink, you commit yourself when you draw, you learn to accept mistakes which inevitably will happen, and you correct things by drawing over, which gives spontaneity and progressive comparison.

The two things to consider initially about the tools are the instrument for drawing and the surface upon which it will be applied. We suggest that beginning students of drawing start with felt tip pens because they are common, available most of the time and easy to use. Many other kinds of pens are sold— quill tip, technical pens such as Castell,

Tools used by Leonardo da Vinci in the 16th Century

36

speedball with various tips, fountain, steel brush, etc. All are good for their intended purpose.

The second prime consideration is the surface, usually a paper of one type or another. The thing to consider with paper is the permeability (whether or not the ink bleeds out or dries rapidly or slowly) and the surface texture (smooth or rough).

Your drawing ability will expand with practice and so will your desire to use a variety of other drawing tools. Ask others about different materials. No better source exists for finding out about the true value of a product than from those who use it. And you will probably learn that quite often the most simple materials are the best. People are often surprised to learn that the best artists rely heavily on felt tip pens and on pencils. Judge whatever tool you use by the desired result you wish to obtain.

The tool always will be only as good as the person using it. The end product depends upon the tool, the surface, and the skill of using both.

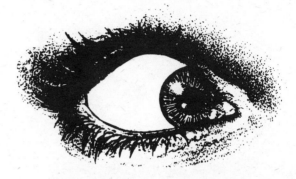

We have heard of a man who lives in a cave and draws with coal on black felt, but we haven't seen any of his work yet.

37

To begin with, probably the best drawing technique to develop first is the use of pure line. We start as children by drawing with lines and we later write with lines. Later, we make the transition to more advanced drawings through the use of line. Line drawing to most people, seems the most natural way to go. It feels comfortable and seems easy to learn.

Line—the best drawing technique.

Illustrated by F. Schonbach, GREFCO, Inc.

Reasons for using the line.

There are at least five good reasons for drawing using simple line:

1. Line is a quick way to visualize ideas with a minimum use of time and materials.

2. Line drawing tools and materials are usually the easiest to use and least expensive.

3. Line is the natural way to draw—children begin with line and adults continue with it as they doodle throughout life.

4. Line emphasizes the basic structure and composition of a drawing which ensures more probable success and a more effective sketch.

5. Line provides a framework on which to hang other drawing techniques such as shading and color.

Scott Bevan

HOW TO PUT IN CONTACT LENSES

ONE — Open lens case.

TWO — Remove lens by touching it with right index finger.

THREE — Grasp lens with thumb and index finger of left hand.

FOUR — Apply one drop of wetting solution to concave surface.

FIVE — Apply one drop to convex surface.

SIX — Flip lens from right index to right middle finger.

SEVEN — Pry eye open with fingers, touch lens to cornea.

EIGHT — Blink.

NINE — Enjoy the scenery. Life is beautiful with contact lenses.

Robert Scott

Line is the basic ingredient of the illustrations on these pages. Notice that the structure and 3-dimensional effect is created almost solely through the use of pure line. What little shading there is, is simply filled in over a drawing that was done with lines—similar to coloring in with crayons as children do.

39

Copy
Copy
Copy
Copy
Cop

"Take pains and pleasure in constantly copying the best things you can find done by the hand of great masters. . . . If you follow the course of one man through constant practice, your intelligence would have to be crude indeed for you not to get some nourishment from it. Then you will find, if nature has granted you any imagination at all, that you will eventually acquire a style individual to yourself, and it cannot help being good; because your hand and your mind, being always accustomed to gather flowers, will ill know how to pluck thorns."

Cerrino Cennini

Copying is an excellent way to learn the skill of drawing. The great art masters studied by copying and by being apprenticed to great artists of their time. Most of them worked in art studios for years before their artistic genius developed to the point where they could stand alone.

You may have heard the admonition not to copy, but that's silly. You learn to talk by copying, you learn to walk by copying; you learn almost all skills by copying something you have seen others do. Why not learn to draw the same way?

Without access and the ability to learn from others, even life's very simple skills would inevitably be difficult to learn.

A variety of different methods of copying can be used to help you learn to draw. The first method involves the use of a grid pattern. This method may seem archaic, but is actually quite useful. It is also quite similar in concept to very popular and standard drawing procedures such as drawing by cubes and drawing through the use of basic shapes, both of which are discussed later in this book.

This is how it's done.

Draw a grid of squares over the item to be copied. Then transfer this same item you are copying by drawing it one square at a time on another surface. If the squares on the second copy are larger or smaller than the squares on the original, then the finished copy will be sized accordingly. If the copy grid is distorted in any way, then the finished copy should also end up distorted.

Copy in order to learn from the best to do the best in a lot less time.

Grid Method

Put your drawing in a grid.

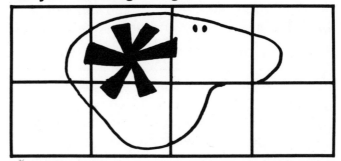

Draw the grid to the size desired—bigger or smaller.

Use the lines on the grid to plot the drawing.

Squares drawn in perspective provide a copy in perspective.

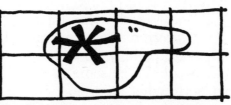

Trace using alot of cheap paper.

Tracing through tissue is also an excellent method of copying. Instead of belaboring a drawing, draw it rough and then refine each step as you trace it through a tissue. The use of tracing paper is also an excellent way to design placement of the component parts in a drawing.

41

Copying Nature

Drawing or copying nature is an excellent way to learn to draw. It makes you more aware, the objects you draw are all "real" (not artificial) and the lighting of the sun yields true shadows or light and dark patterns.

Try tracing nature through a glass held in front of you. Make sure that the glass is steady in place so that your images will not be distorted. Then simply trace what you see through the glass. Use a grease pencil or crayon-type pencil which will adhere to the glass surface. This method of actually tracing nature is a form of true drawing. Drawing is simply the transfer of the image of an object into linear form on a flat (two-dimensional) surface. Whether you trace nature through a clear piece of glass or "trace" the image on a piece of paper held in front of you, the principle is the same. You are just drawing exactly what you see.

Collect a drawing file.

You will probably find it educational and helpful to begin collecting a file of different drawing and illustrating techniques that appeal to you. All good artists find it essential to their profession to subscribe to the latest magazines. They usually keep copies of art award winners also.

You will be able to "borrow" another person's successful technique by studying it. You should not plagiarize or steal their work, but it is helpful to see what they are doing. New and exciting approaches surface in the art world each year and it will inspire you to be able to "pick the brain" of the best by collecting and studying their work.

You will find it beneficial to see how others have solved similar drawing problems to those you will encounter. By referring to your file, you can see what they do in a given situation. The file won't draw it for you, but it will certainly show you how it has been done by others.

Nature is the greatest teacher

Use what others have done as a step into your own drawings

42

Copy as a helper— not as a permanent crutch!

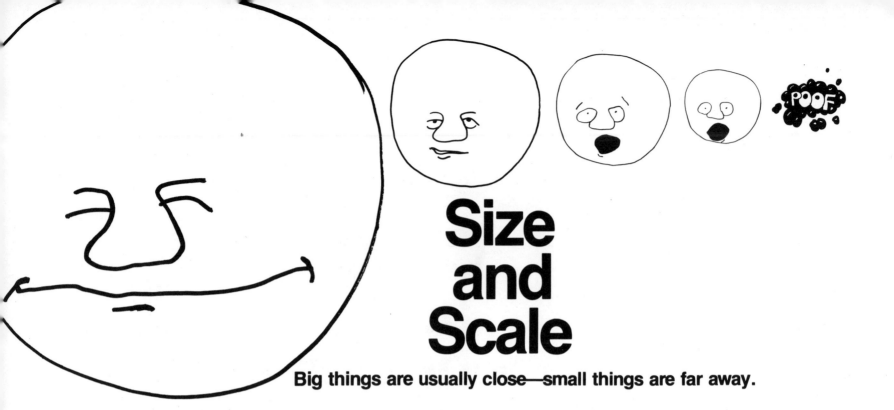

Size
and
Scale

Big things are usually close—small things are far away.

Drawing, for the most part, is the ability to create the illusion of depth and dimension on a two-dimensional surface. And one of the primary factors that indicates to our mind "size" is that the closer things are, the larger they look. Notice the circular faces at the top of this page—the larger one looks closer and the smaller ones look farther away.

It is important to also realize that the illusion of size and depth are best portrayed when there is comparison with an object of a known size. If we were to draw a small picture of a man next to a larger man it would usually automatically cause our mind to assume that the small man was far away. If we were to draw a picture of a small sphere next to a larger identical sphere, our mind would assume that the smaller sphere was farther away. A single sphere drawn, however, often wouldn't tell us its relative size or distance at all. It would be just a large, small or medium

size sphere to us. Place a man next to the sphere and we would immediately recognize its size. Comparison indicates to our mind an object's size and its distance from us if compared to an identical object or an object of known size.

Watch a newborn baby whose eyes have developed enough so that he can distinguish objects passing in front of him. If you move an object in his line of vision, he may sometimes flinch when the object is some distance away where it is no danger to him; or conversely, he may keep his eyes wide open when the object is so close that it would cause you or me to blink. He has no concept of where the objects are in relation to himself. As he grows older, he learns when things are close or far away. He learns that an object of standard size appears to be larger when it is close to him and appears to grow smaller as it moves away.

44

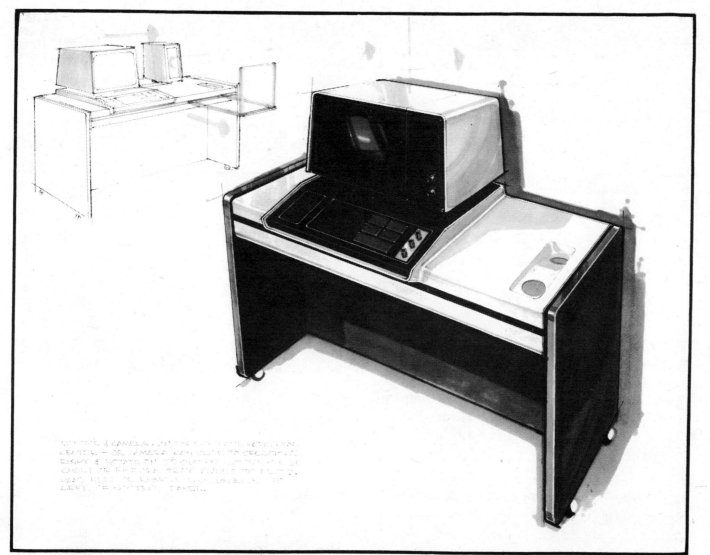

David
Edwards

Tucker P. Madawick, division vice president, Industrial Design Department, RCA

These objects show how size indicates depth, distance and scale to our mind. The television-like terminals indicate that one is closer because it is larger. And we know that the larger monster is closer than his smaller counterpart. Indeed his hand is quite close for it appears much larger than the rest of his body.

45

A good sketching exercise is to take a common small object, such as a pen, and draw it while changing its surroundings to make it seem much larger than its real size.

If objects of known sizes are placed out of their normal visual context it does strange things to our visual perception. This helps us see, draw and think in different ways that normal. It gets us out of a rut and helps us see and experience things in a different light.

We all automatically interpret drawings such as the ones shown here as being comical or absurd. Everyone knows that a pen is smaller

than a person, that a marker is not pulled by an army of slaves, or that an air cleaner is not a huge walking machine. But the drawings get us looking at our world from another point of view simply by changing scale and size.

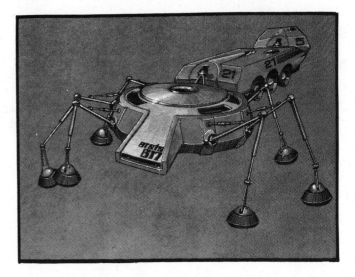

The next page shows the importance of placing objects of known size in an illustration. By having a person next to the trees or buildings we can determine their sizes. One lone tree, however, would be confusing to our minds because we would have no idea of its real size.

Use size distortion as a technique for emphasis.

Human figures in drawings give the viewer relative sizes of the other objects and spaces in the picture.

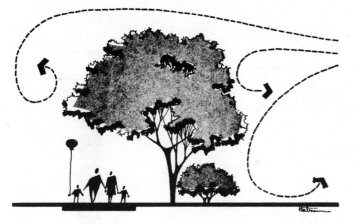

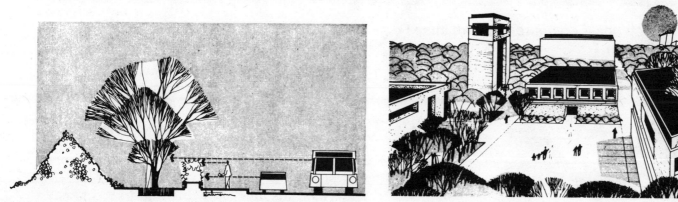

Plants/People/and Environmental Quality, U.S. Government Publication

47

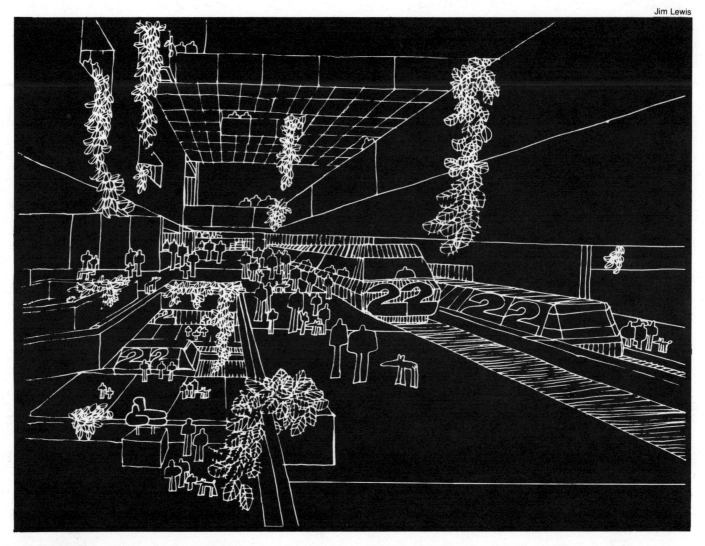

To establish scale compare a known shape to an unknown.

The immensity of the building above becomes obvious when people are included (above).

The illustration to the left shows how the comparison of an unfamiliar object to one of a known size quickly communicates valuable information to our minds. To say that Saudi Arabia covers 872,722 square miles means little. But to place a map of Saudi Arabia over a silhouette of the United States tells an American instantly how big Saudi Arabia is.

48

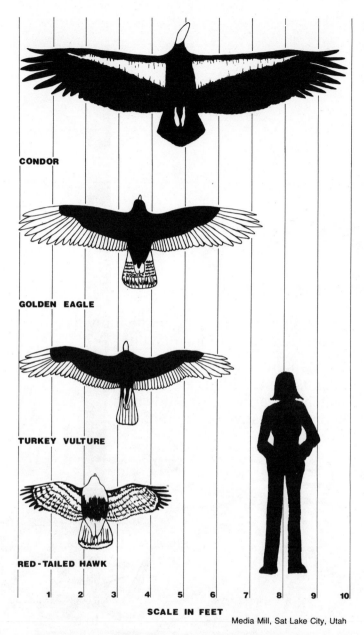

CONDOR

GOLDEN EAGLE

TURKEY VULTURE

RED-TAILED HAWK

1 2 3 4 5 6 7 8 9 10

SCALE IN FEET

Media Mill, Sat Lake City, Utah

All birds are small until we compare these unique varieties with a known size such as that of a man. Then some of these fowl creatures become rather large.

This rectangle means little to us when no comparison is available.

But place a lady nearby and it becomes about the size of a desk.

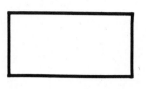

A Volkswagen beetle transforms it into a garage.

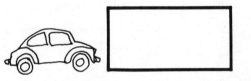

And a truck chassis makes it the size of a moving van.

Size is relative when it comes to drawing. It depends upon our knowledge of the size of its surroundings.

49

Overlapping

Put things in front of other things

Overlapping is a valuable component of good drawing. Overlapping gives scale, provides depth, produces unity and interest and gives direction to a drawing.

The overlapping of items in a drawing gives relationship, a more comfortable feeling,

direction and dimension to the individual component parts of the drawing.

Overlapping creates the illusion of depth. It tells us which things are closer and which are farther away. It lets us know the relative position of things.

David Edwards

Overlapping gives scale, depth, unity and interest.

United States
Steel Corp.

50

Architects/Planners Alliance, Salt Lake City, Utah

Scale or relative size of objects is made more obvious by overlapping.

A drawing is more unified if items in it overlap. A setting or drawing holds together better, its parts relate better and it appears more comfortable if component parts overlap. Notice that we live in an overlapping world. Everything is in-front-of or behind something else. It "feels right" to have items in our visual field overlapping. Also notice that good art overlaps and groups things in order to create a better composition.

**Don't be afraid to cover up parts of a good
drawing in order to give it added depth.**

Aluminum Company of
America, Corporate
Design Division

Your interest is enhanced if a drawing
employs overlapping. Items that lie on top of,
sit in front of, wrap around, or lean against
something are generally more interesting to
look at. And overlapping intensifies
curiousity—you wonder about the total when
you can see only a part.

OVERLAPPING

Overlapping, to be an effective tool, must first have all things in the picture roughly sketched as if they were transparent—as if you could see through them. The objects are first drawn as if they were made out of glass. By beginning with transparent objects it is easy to see if they have been correctly drawn. In the finished drawing all objects will be correctly drawn.

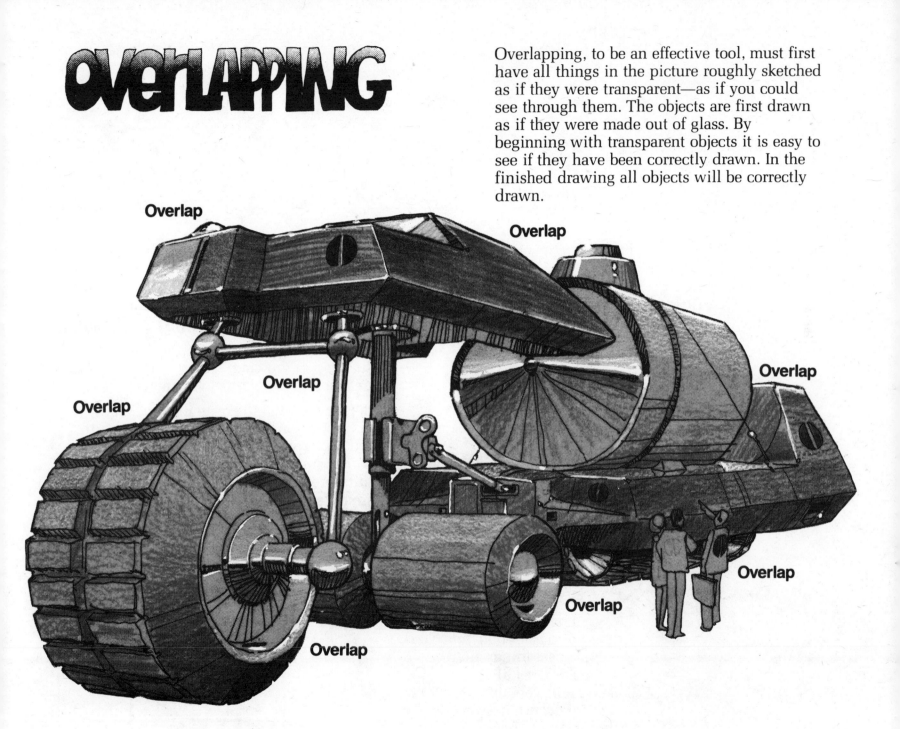

Overlap

Overlap

Overlap

Overlap

Overlap

Overlap

Overlap

Overlap

Overlap

Detail

. . . unless detail is placed into a structured pattern, it is rapidly forgotten.
Edward A. Hamilton

Detail is a helpful component to rapid visualization drawing. It emphasizes necessary points and gives pizzaz to a drawing.

Detail is essential to create the illusion of reality. As mentioned on previous pages, the mind "interprets" what it sees. And a little detail at strategic points helps lead the mind to interpret "reality" into the drawing.

With detail you can draw attention to the important parts of the drawing you want people to see.

HOW TO APPLY EYE-DROPS

VISINE

TILT HEAD BACK

POSITION BOTTLE OVER EYE

SQUEEZE

REPEAT OVER OTHER EYE

Terry Ipsen

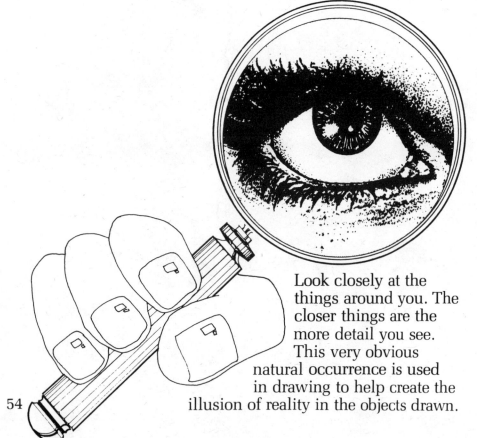

Look closely at the things around you. The closer things are the more detail you see. This very obvious natural occurrence is used in drawing to help create the illusion of reality in the objects drawn.

54

HOME-MADE SMALL ELECTRICAL GENERATOR

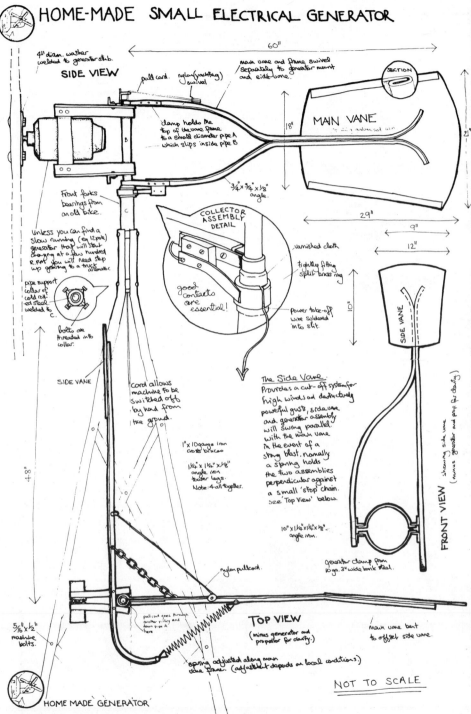

4" diam. washer welded to generator stub.

SIDE VIEW

pull cord. nylon (yachting) swivel.

60"

Main vane and frame swivel separately to generator mount and side vane.

SECTION

18"

21"

MAIN VANE

clamp holds the top of the vane frame to a small diameter pipe A which slips inside pipe B

Front forks bearings from old bike.

3/4" x 3/4" x 1/8" angle.

29"

9"

12"

COLLECTOR ASSEMBLY DETAIL

Unless you can find a slow running (eg 12 pole) generator that will start charging at a few hundred R.P.M. you will need step up gearing to a truck alternator.

varnished cloth

tightly fitting split brass ring.

good contacts are essential!

power take-off wire soldered into slit.

pipe support collar of cold rolled steel welded to C.

10"

bolts are threaded into collar.

SIDE VANE

cord allows machine to be switched off by hand from the ground.

The Side Vane.
Provides a cut-off system for high winds and destructively powerful gusts, side vane and generator assembly will swing parallel with the main vane in the event of a strong blast. normally a spring holds the two assemblies perpendicular against a small 'stop chain'. see 'Top View' below.

SIDE VANE

1" x 10 gauge iron cross braces

1¼ x 1½" x 1/8" angle iron tower legs. Note: 4-all together.

48"

10" x 1¼" x 1¼" x 1/8" angle iron.

nylon pullcord.

Generator clamp from 10 ga. 3" wide bank steel.

5/8 x 1/2" machine bolts.

pull cord goes through another pulley and down pipe A here

TOP VIEW
(minus generator and propeller for clarity.)

Main vane bent to offset side vane.

spring adjusted along main vane frame. (adjustment depends on local conditions.)

FRONT VIEW (showing side vane) (minus generator and prop for clarity.)

NOT TO SCALE

HOME MADE GENERATOR

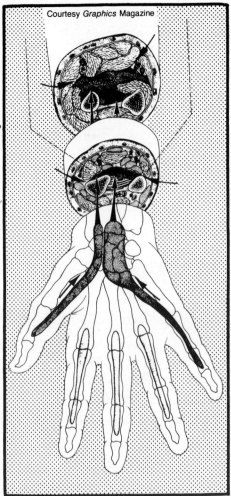

Courtesy *Graphics* Magazine

Without intricate detail, medical illustrations would be relatively worthless.

Inserting small areas in a drawing helps to explain, in visual language, more of the drawing. The small electrical generator contains inlaid details which strengthen the communicative value of the drawing.

55

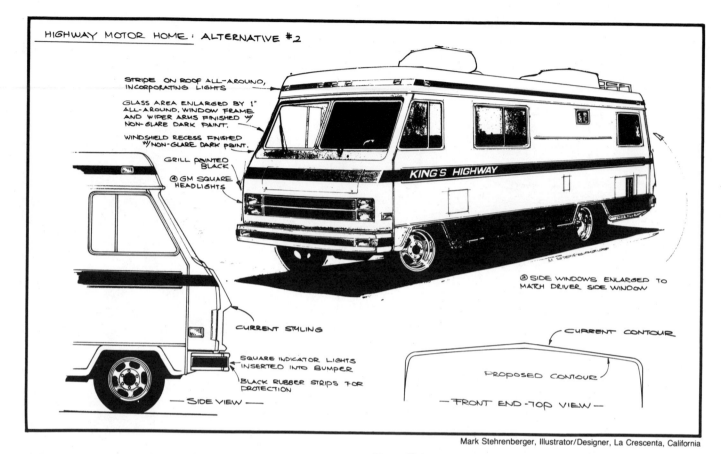

HIGHWAY MOTOR HOME: ALTERNATIVE #2

STRIPE ON ROOF ALL-AROUND, INCORPORATING LIGHTS

GLASS AREA ENLARGED BY 1" ALL-AROUND. WINDOW FRAME AND WIPER ARMS FINISHED W/ NON-GLARE DARK PAINT.

WINDSHIELD RECESS FINISHED W/ NON-GLARE DARK PAINT.

GRILL PAINTED BLACK

④ GM SQUARE HEADLIGHTS

KING'S HIGHWAY

② SIDE WINDOWS ENLARGED TO MATCH DRIVER SIDE WINDOW

CURRENT STYLING

SQUARE INDICATOR LIGHTS INSERTED INTO BUMPER

BLACK RUBBER STRIPS FOR PROTECTION

— SIDE VIEW —

CURRENT CONTOUR

PROPOSED CONTOUR

— FRONT END - TOP VIEW —

Mark Stehrenberger, Illustrator/Designer, La Crescenta, California

The placement of detail within this room scene makes it more realistic.

Levolor Inc.

Detail is more important to rapid visualization because of its ability to emphasize a given point.

Detail allows us to understand the stinger mechanism of a Black Widow spider.

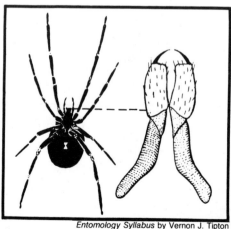

Entomology Syllabus by Vernon J. Tipton

56

Detail is essential for the explicit communication of complicated material. It emphasizes points and simplifies.

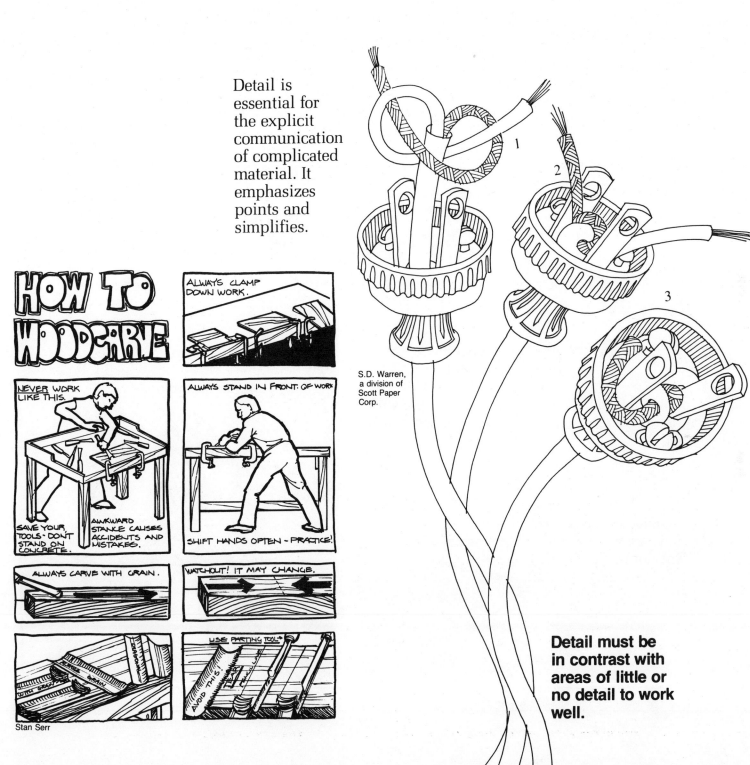

S.D. Warren, a division of Scott Paper Corp.

Detail must be in contrast with areas of little or no detail to work well.

57

Contour

Contour or wrap-around lines can indicate shape or volume.

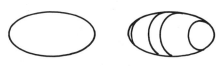

Contour lines give volume to the oval. The one on the left looks flat, like a cut-out piece of paper—while the one at the right seems to be shaped like an egg.

Draw an object with the use of contour lines. It is an easy exercise to try. Simply begin to draw something with lines which follow different contours of the object.

Notice that lines can create a three-dimensional look. The illustrations done here are the work of computers and doodlers. But notice the depth and volume.

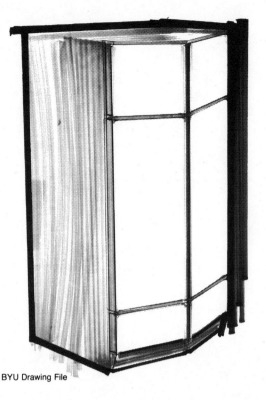

The head is an example of contour drawing which demonstrates the apparent volume derived from simple lines. The slanted lines of the box-like structure indicate that it has a pointed or "V" shaped front.

When drawing contour lines you should become conscious of your hand holding the pen and its pressure against the paper. Don't just draw the lines over the shape, feel them. Whether it is a car or a face, use your eye and hand to feel the contour line as it caresses the surface. Sense the contour as it travels down, around and into the picture exerting pressure on the paper as needed. With contour lines, more than any other technique, you must respond to that two dimensional sketch as an actual three dimensional object. Feel it!

59

The dimension here is primarily a result of
contour lines. Especially notice the importance
of the lines on the door of the automobile.
These curved lines give a protruding depth to
the view of the side of the car.

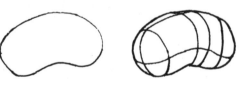

**Draw a shape. Then with wrap-around lines
make it into a volume.**

60

Drawing file, Brigham Young University,
Design Department

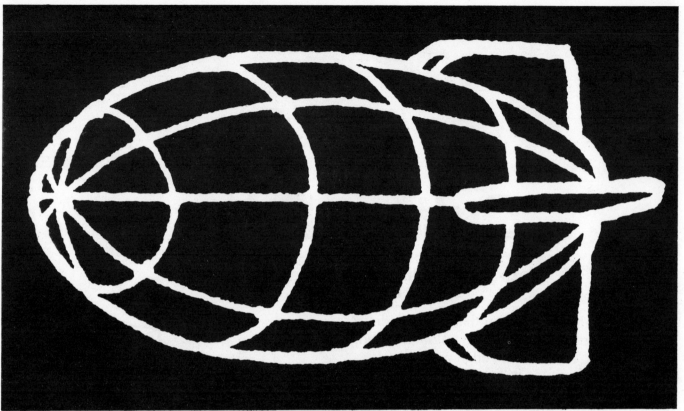

Scott Bevan

A lack of contour lines would make the blimp flat.

Define the shape with a contour line.

Practice drawing contour lines by drawing lines over old magazine pictures. Find photos of objects and sketch lines over their surfaces.

If you are having problems with a shape that just doesn't look right, draw some contour lines lightly over it. It will surprise you how well the lines will help you see the way the shape should be drawn.

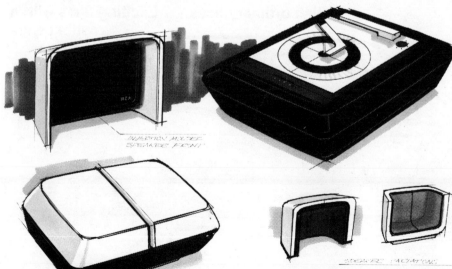

Industrial Design Department, RCA

61

Cutting Edge

Make the edge lines darker than the inner lines.

It is a natural phenomenon that the outside edges of all objects seem to be bolder and more pronounced. This outside edge we call a cutting edge because it "cuts" the object into its relative space. By making the outside edge of each part of a drawing darker and bolder, the drawing takes on a more real and believable appearance.

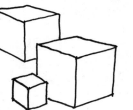 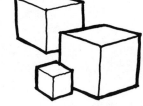

Blah ordinary lines   **Exciting lines with a cutting edge**

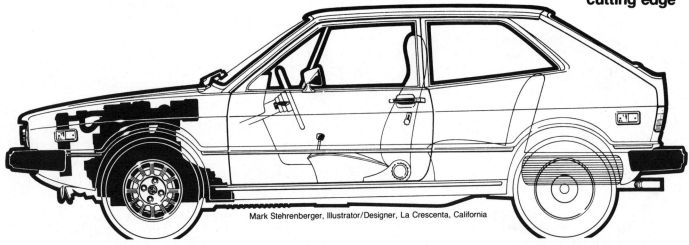

Mark Stehrenberger, Illustrator/Designer, La Crescenta, California

These drawings all employ the use of a bold cutting edge. Notice how crisp, clean and believable the edge makes the drawings.

Stan Serr

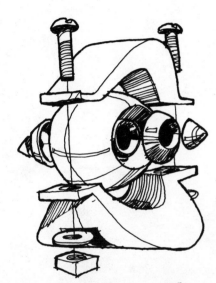

Look at your surroundings and notice how the outside edges seem to be more vivid and make the object "stand out." All lines of any object are important, but the outside "cutting edge" appears to be more pronounced than all other lines most of the time.

Western Wood Products Association

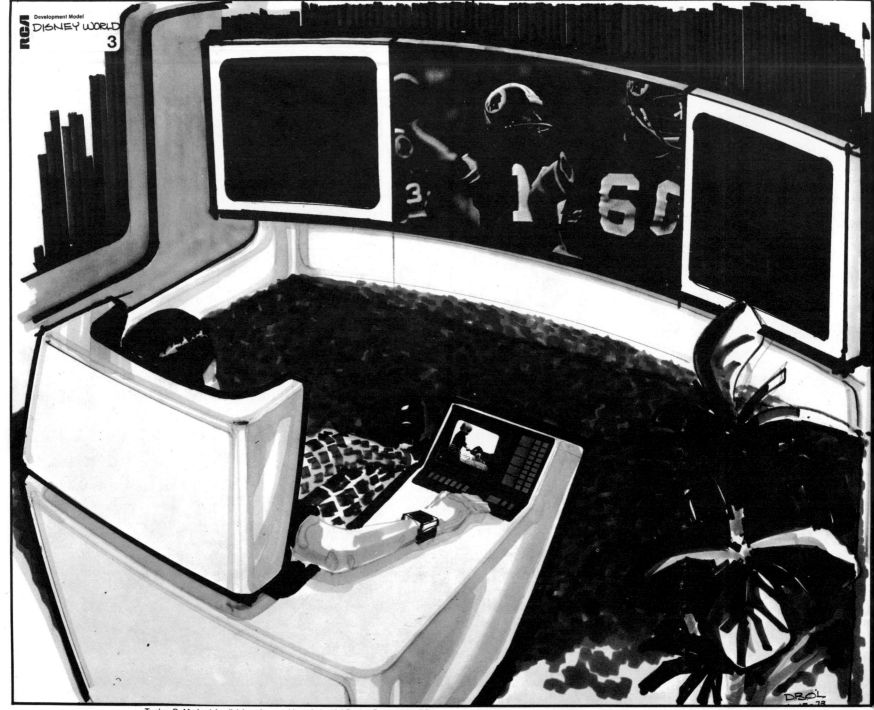

Tucker P. Madawick, division vice president, Industrial Design Department, RCA

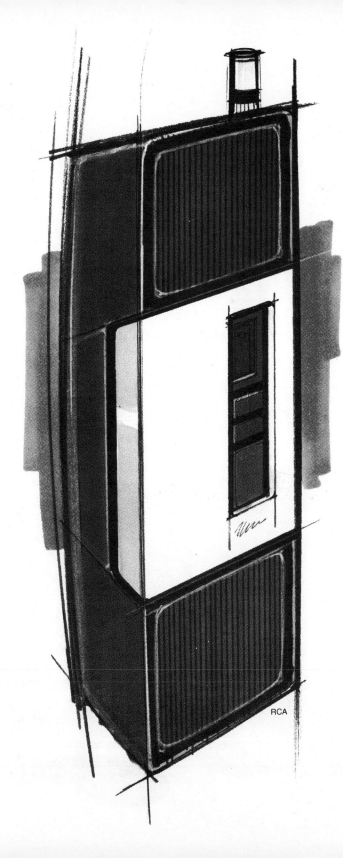

RCA

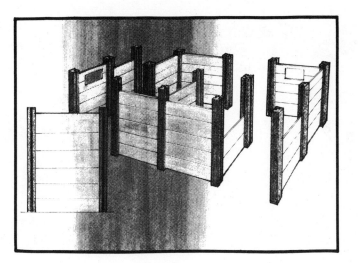

Drawing by Ronald and Carolyn Nuetzel, Design contest winners, Reynolds Aluminum

It is possibly this "cutting edge" phenomenon that leads all of us to want to draw the outside dimensions of an object first. If you are like us, you have a natural tendency to silhouette the drawn object first.

Use a bold outer line to show the shape through space.

The keys to shade and shadow are the sun (or other light source) and its direction and angle.

Shade and Shadow

Shading and shadows give volume to a shape and make it more interesting.

Shading and shadows in drawings are often overlooked and their importance forgotten. But if there is enough light for you to see an object there is shading and a shadow present.

Shading is the varying degree of value from light to dark which is created on an object by the light which strikes the angled and curved planes of that object. All objects have varying degrees of value of shaded portions.

Subtle variations in lighting can create many degrees of shading on a single object. You may find it helpful to mentally simplify the shading by thinking of it as having only four values—light, light gray, dark gray and dark. These four variations should be sufficient to provide shading for most drawings.

On a rounded surface, such as a sphere or cylinder, these shaded areas blend gradually from light to dark.

Cast shadow is the darkest portion on the drawing of an object. It is darker than any surface of the object because it receives less reflected light than do the surfaces of the object.

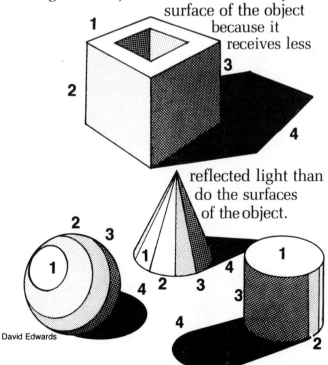

David Edwards

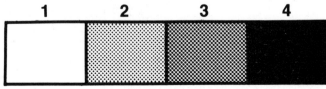

66

The length and direction of the light source forms a triangle which has the shadow as its base. This imaginary triangle is an easy method for establishing the shadow of any object.

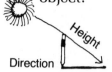

The height of the light source dictates the angle of the triangle which forms the cast shadow.

The height of the light source determines the length of the shadow and its direction.

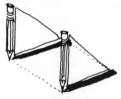

All shadows are indicators of the height and direction of their light source.

Solid objects (walls, plane surfaces, etc.) form cast shadows in the same manner as a single pencil.

Shadows often look complicated and difficult to draw, but they aren't. The simple illustrations on this page show that the triangle method is easy to use and fool-proof. Triangles form the basis for all shadows. In order to draw the cast shadow find the light source and determine the triangle formed.

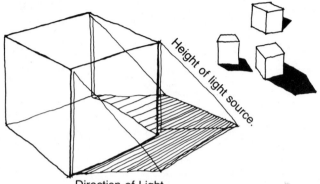

Make a shadow that complements the shape rather than detracts from it.

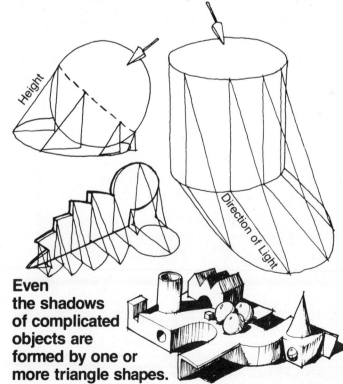

Even the shadows of complicated objects are formed by one or more triangle shapes.

**Lightly draw your drawing then proceed from
dark to light with the shading.**

68

Pencil Broadsides, Theodore Kautzky, Van Nostrand Reinhold Co.

One popular method of drawing is to start with the dark areas and move gradually to the lighter areas. By looking at these drawings you can readily see how illustrated objects gradually evolve from dark and light masses. Most people find, when they try drawing the shadow and shaded images first, that this is a new, relatively effortless and simple way to draw that produces quality results.

Notice especially in Kautzsky's drawing of a tree that almost no lines exist. Limbs are drawn not with lines, but with shadow or absence of shadow. Usually a happy medium exists—some line and some shadow. Previous pages have shown that lines can stand alone and this shows that shadow can also stand alone.

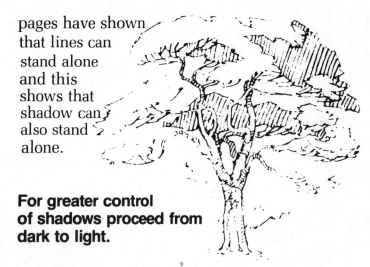

For greater control of shadows proceed from dark to light.

69

70

Mark Stehrenberger

In real life, shadows and shading are as much a part of visual objects as the objects themselves. These areas of light and dark values can, by themselves, form shapes and images. The drawings on these two facing pages are examples of strong shadows and shading.

To help you see what shadows are doing, squint your eyes and notice just the dark areas. These dark areas are the most dominant part of any drawing and squinting is a good "trick" which enables you to better isolate them.

Scott Bevan

71

Shape

A tree visually is seen as a solid in space, but an artist consciously may invert the world to see the tree as a hole carved within a solid block of air.

W. J. J. Gordon

Negative and positive shapes are a natural extension of shadows. What you see may actually be what you don't see.

Strange as it sounds, what we fail to see is often more meaningful than what we see. The illustrations on these pages indicate the visual strength of negative and positive shapes.

No line here, but your eye draws it in.

You need the apple to see the bite!

William E. Borden

72

When negative and positive shapes are used to illustrate a point, caution should be used to choose the most meaningful shape possible. The two silhouettes of the cowboy are the same person seen in the same running position, but from two different angles. The drawing on the left is self-explanatory and

meaningful—you can easily see what is happening. The one on the right, however, is a confusing ink spot. Without the two silhouettes for comparison, you wouldn't be able to distinguish or understand the righthand drawing.

It's not only what you see that matters but also what you don't see.

The consideration for all drawings should be that the view which tells the most complete story should be the one drawn. A simple method to use in determining the best view is to imagine the drawing as a positive or negative shape. View the object as something cut out of the background so that all you see is the void left.

The negative and positive shapes give a reasonably complete view of the illustration below.

Make both your negative and positive shapes interesting.

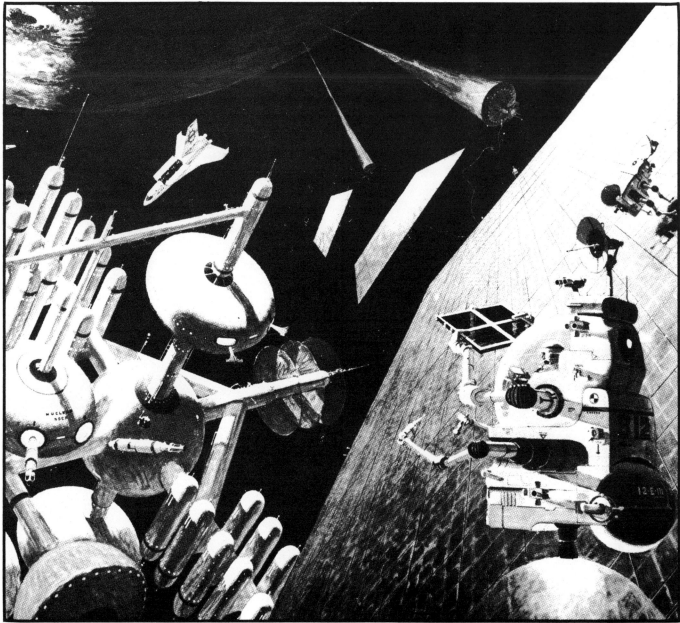

By Robert McCall, Washington, D.C. in *Arizona Highways*, August 1975

Both the dark and the light areas of a drawing tell a story. This illustration forcefully uses negative and positive shapes simultaneously. The background is as important to this drawing as the space vehicles themselves. The use of the total area of the drawing, including the background, makes the illustration more interesting, real and vivid.

These drawings were done almost entirely through the use of negative and positive shapes. Lines are implied where no lines exist (the back of the truck and around the headlights and front bumper). And yet the strength of the shapes carries the drawing, even when the background and the drawing act as one continuous area.

Concept Design Associates, Salt Lake City, Utah

Perspective

David Edwards

Parallel lines converge at a common point on the horizon.
The Perspective Rule

Items in our view of the natural world seem to get smaller and smaller and vanish in the distance. This view of a diminishing world is called perspective and is created in drawings through the use of vanishing points and horizon lines. You have undoubtedly seen a string of telephone poles or railroad tracks which vividly illustrate the phenomenon. When items of equal size are placed in parallel lines going away from you it is very easy to see how they apparently diminish in size and seem to vanish in the distance. The drawing shown here is an example of one point perspective.

76

B.C. Discovers Perspective

B.C. by permission of Johnny Hart and Field Enterprises, Inc.

To create perspective in drawing a vanishing point is used. It works on the principle that parallel lines grow closer together and get gradually smaller until they vanish at a point on the horizon. If you are looking at something, then your eye determines where the vanishing point sits on the horizon. If you are drawing a picture then you determine where the vanishing point touches the horizon.

Hold a clear piece of glass or plexiglass stationary between you and an object. Now take a felt pen and trace what you see. If you are careful, and the glass is held completely stationary, you will end up with an excellent drawing in perfect perspective.

A good artist does exactly what you have done except that he usually draws on an opaque surface which he holds lower in front of him. He simply has learned to "trace" things on his drawing surface without the necessity of it being transparent.

Hold a clear, hard surface in front of you and trace what you see. Be sure the surface is completely stationary.

Draw the same object from different points of view. By varying your angle of view you will be able to clearly see the subtle changes in perspective.

To help you visualize the relationship between vanishing points and horizon lines imagine yourself standing in water up to your eyes. You can see both above the water and below the water at the same time. At a point on the surface of the water and way in the distance, all things seem to disappear. This imaginary water surface is the horizon line and the point where all things disappear is the vanishing point.

The horizon line, which is the surface of your imaginary body of water, is always horizontal and level. Just as water is always level, so is your horizon line.

The cube will change depending on your point of view.

78

One Point Perspective

All the drawings on this page are examples of one point perspective. When objects are seen as though you were looking directly at them (straight on), they seem to diminish in size to the edges farthest from your vision. This diminishing size creates the illusion that the object would grow gradually smaller to a single point where it vanishes at the horizon.

Western Wood Products Association

Notice that all the lines, except the vertical and horizontal lines, point toward a vanishing point. The vertical and horizontal lines always remain parallel.

Drawing in perspective is a relatively easy task once you understand the principles. Drawing one point perspective is the simplest and therefore a good starting point.

One point perspective uses three kinds of lines—horizontal, vertical and perspective.

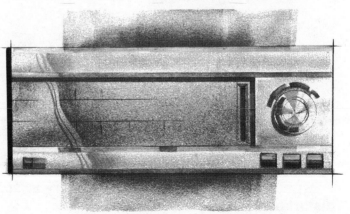

79

Perspective is something we are all very aware of especially when we try to figure out the distortion in this optical illusion.

Two Point Perspective

Two point perspective uses two kinds of lines—vertical and perspective.

two vanishing points are, the less the degree of convergence of the sides of the boxes.

All vertical lines remain parallel just as in one point perspective, but there are no horizontal lines.

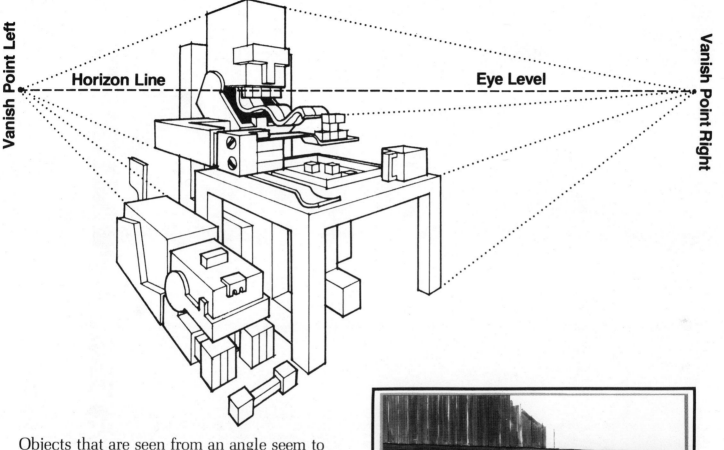

Vanish Point Left

Horizon Line　　　　　　　　　**Eye Level**

Vanish Point Right

Objects that are seen from an angle seem to diminish in size in two directions. Notice how the illustration above diminishes in size in two directions as the sides of the objects get farther away from you.

This is accomplished by having two vanishing points, for drawing purposes, located one at each side of the paper. Both points are located on the same horizon line. The farther apart the

Concept Design Associates, Salt Lake City, Utah

81

These drawings are modifications of one point perspective. Notice that all horizontal and vertical lines are parallel and that perspective lines head toward the vanishing point.

Scott Bevan

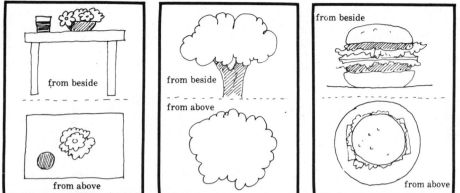

from beside

from above

from beside

from above

from beside

from above

Know how an object looks from the various views before you draw it.

To become proficient at perspective it is necessary that you observe objects from various points of view. See things from the top, from the sides and from the bottom. Each viewpoint gives the observer a new understanding of the object. In perspective you must then take the flat views of the object and construct it in space as a three dimensional shape.

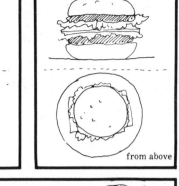

Learning Through Play, Jean Marzollo and Janice Lloyd, Harper & Row, Publishers, Inc.

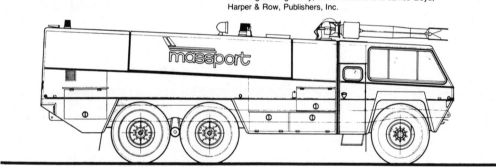

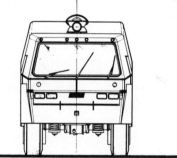

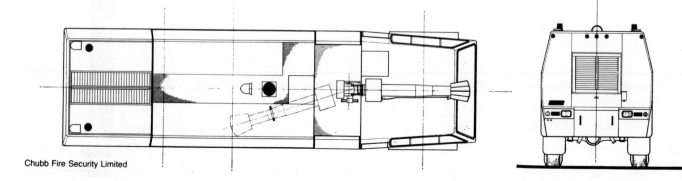

Chubb Fire Security Limited

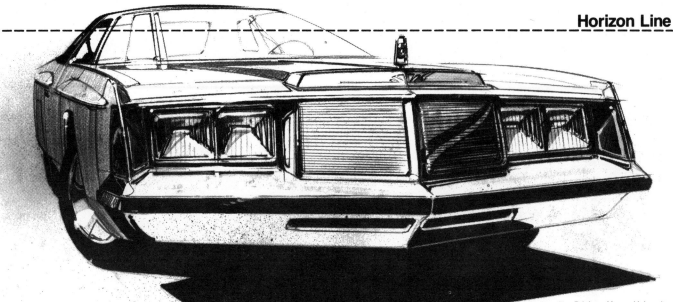

Drawing file, Brigham Young University,
Design Department

Next time you are in front of a parked automobile, bend down and look at the car with your eye-level about the height shown above. You will be surprised at the details you hadn't noticed before. Or get up on a chair and look around. Just a small change of eye-level literally changes our image of the world around us.

SWIVEL

DEFLECTED
SOUNT

long piece
plastic

but fiberboard
cover.

Industrial Design Department, RCA

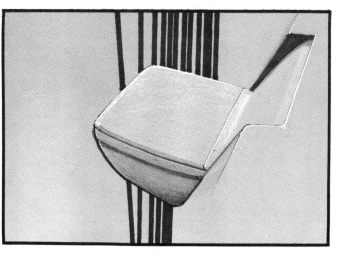

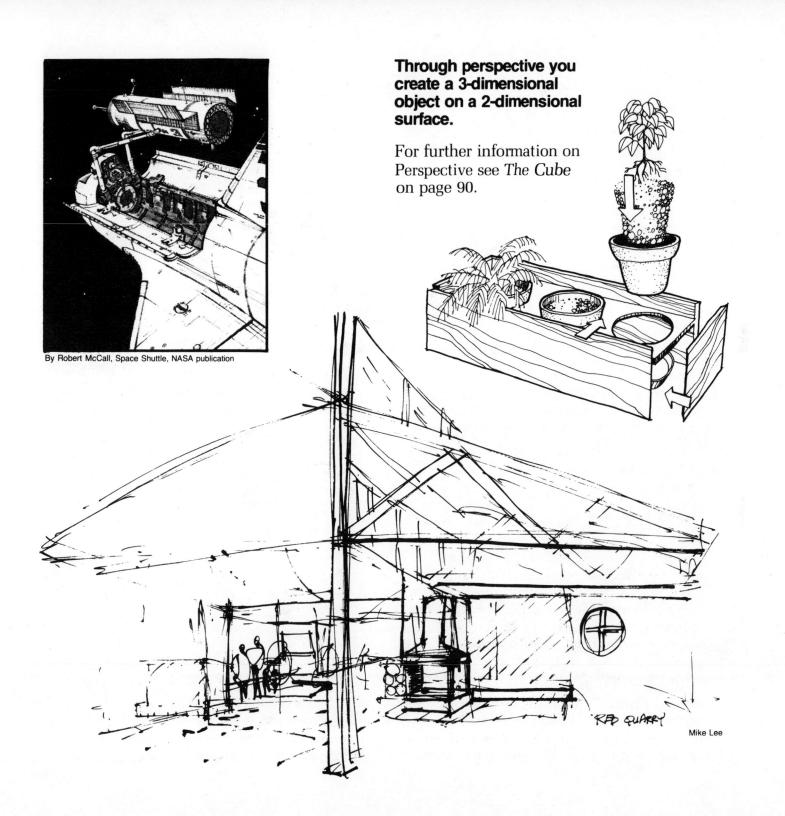

By Robert McCall, Space Shuttle, NASA publication

Through perspective you create a 3-dimensional object on a 2-dimensional surface.

For further information on Perspective see *The Cube* on page 90.

RED QUARRY

Mike Lee

85

Geometric Origin

All objects are based upon four basic shapes—the cube, the sphere, the cylinder and the cone.

Using basic shapes helps us draw quickly and accurately. By breaking complex shapes down into simple geometric forms, we can draw them more easily.

Drawing with the help of basic geometric shapes requires the acquisition of two skills. First is learning to give basic shapes an appearance of dimension and depth—making them look three-dimensional. And second is being able to visualize a complex number of simpler shapes which are connected to form the more complex one.

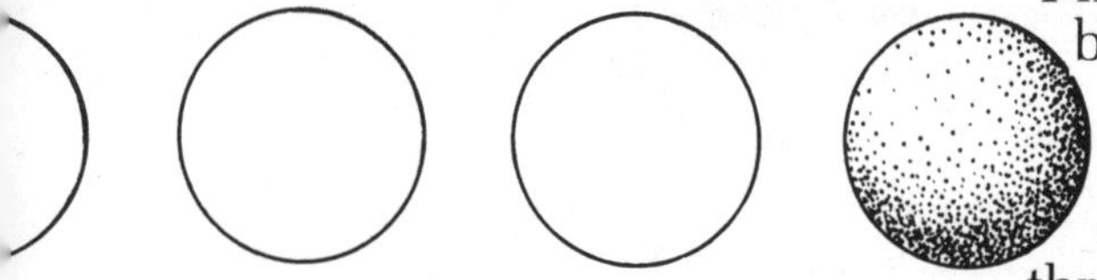

The illusion of dimension and depth are achieved primarily with the assistance of shading, shadows, contour lines and perspective. Shading transforms the circle shown here into a sphere. The shape is the same—the circle—but one appears to be two-dimensional and flat while the other appears to have volume.

Cube, Cylinder, Sphere, Cone.

When an individual learns to see a complex object as a combination of the basic shapes shown here, he is on his way to being able to draw accurately and well. It is quite simple to add detail once the form is made.

86

Cube

Building
Toy box
Garage
Shoe box
Truck
Desk
Van
End Table

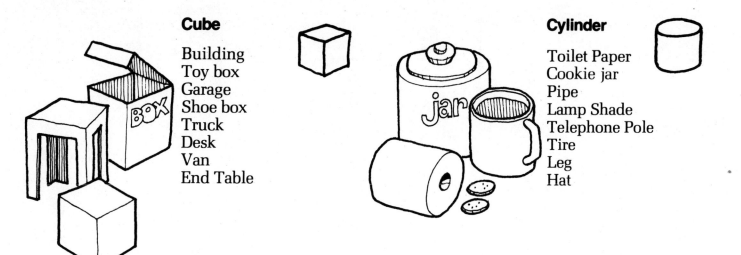

The cube is the most often used basic shape. Further into the book we'll show you how to use the cube as a basis for a great deal of your drawing.

Cylinder

Toilet Paper
Cookie jar
Pipe
Lamp Shade
Telephone Pole
Tire
Leg
Hat

The sphere and circular shapes are the basis for a great many objects which you might not expect. Body joints are an example of the use of this basic shape in drawing.

Sphere

Basket Ball
Pumpkin
Rock
Football Helmet
Head
Light Bulb
Door Knob
World

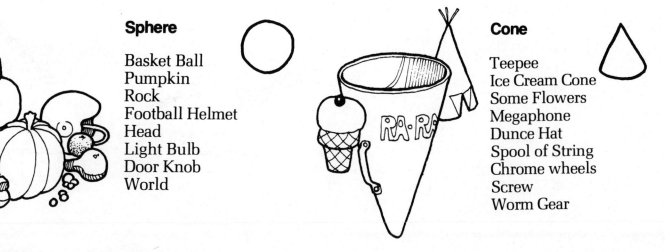

Cone

Teepee
Ice Cream Cone
Some Flowers
Megaphone
Dunce Hat
Spool of String
Chrome wheels
Screw
Worm Gear

The cylinder is used a great deal in mechanical and architectural applications. Many man-made objects are cylindrical. Plants and trees also employ the cylinder shape.

The cone is probably least often noticed in its pure form. You will find that it is used extensively in drawing, however, for such things as arms and legs and the like.

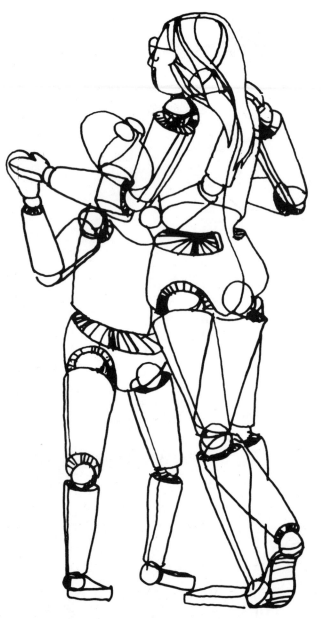

The cube, or a variation of it, forms the basis for the chair. Drawing the legs would be very difficult without the cube shape to help place them with correct perspective. The basic cubical shape provides the necessary guidelines within which the chair can be drawn.

You can draw *anything* by using the four basic shapes to form a basis and simplify the drawing. Look around and notice the basic shapes. Even though some are obvious in your surroundings, most objects that occur in real life are a combination of the shapes or derivatives of them and are less obvious.

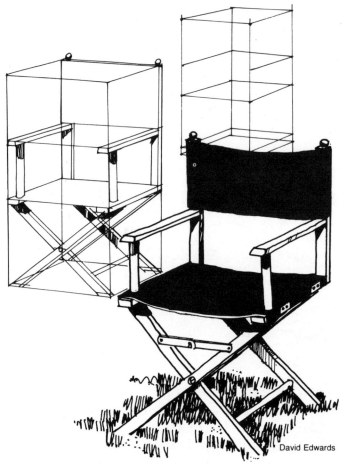

David Edwards

You can draw anything by using the four basic shapes.

Notice the extensive use of spheres and conical shapes. The head and joints are all spheres and the limbs are all elongated cones.

Now look carefully at your surroundings. Try to imagine things as having been put together with basic shapes. It may take a little time for you to be able to visualize basic shapes but with a little practice it will soon become quite natural.

Try this exercise. Go through a magazine and draw the basic shape skeleton of the objects you see. It won't take long, but will give you a quick working knowledge of geometric origins of objects. The best teacher is experience.

Most people don't realize that drawings evolve. People assume that an artist can sit down and draw a finished product. An artist's drawings evolve from a simple to a more complex and finished stage.

Basic shapes are structures for drawing. They serve much the same purpose as our skeletons

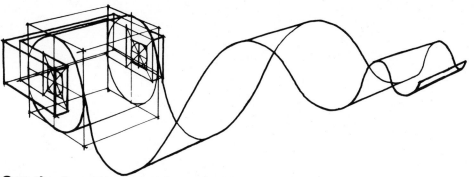

See the transparent structure of the object or space before you draw the outer surface.

do to hold our bodies in the correct posture. Or the same as scaffolding does to help build a skyscraper. Without basic shapes in drawing, our illustrations would be misshapen, distorted, out of perspective and generally wrong. The use of a basic shape skeleton is necessary for accurate freehand drawing.

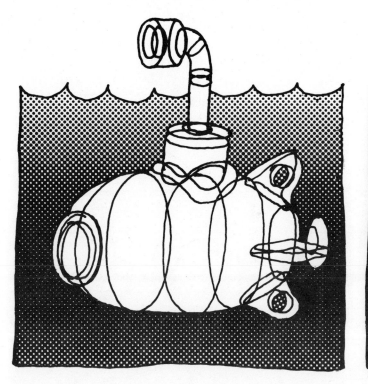

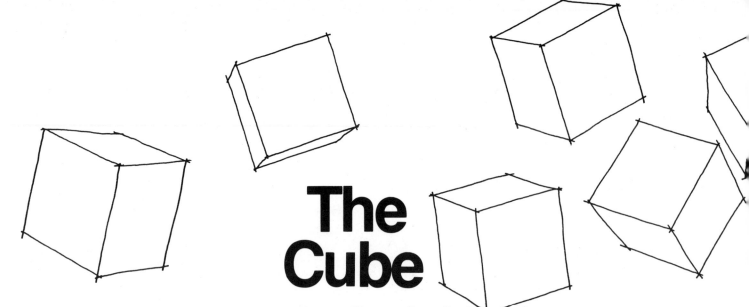

The Cube

A secret formula for drawing any three dimensional objects in space.

1 point 2 point 3 point

If you were required to choose one basic shape for all drawing, the cube would be your best choice. All other basic shapes can be drawn in correct perspective by using the cube as a guide. These next few pages show you how.

First, as a reminder, notice the cubes below within the circles. One point perspective is drawn with three different kinds of lines—parallel vertical lines, parallel horizontal lines and perspective lines. Two point perspective is drawn with two different kinds of lines—parallel vertical lines and perspective lines which go toward either of two vanishing points. Three point perspective is drawn with only one kind of line—perspective lines which go toward any of three separate vanishing points. All vanishing points are placed on a horizon line (eye level

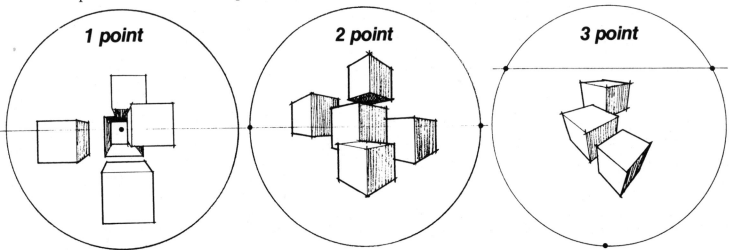

1 point   *2 point*   *3 point*

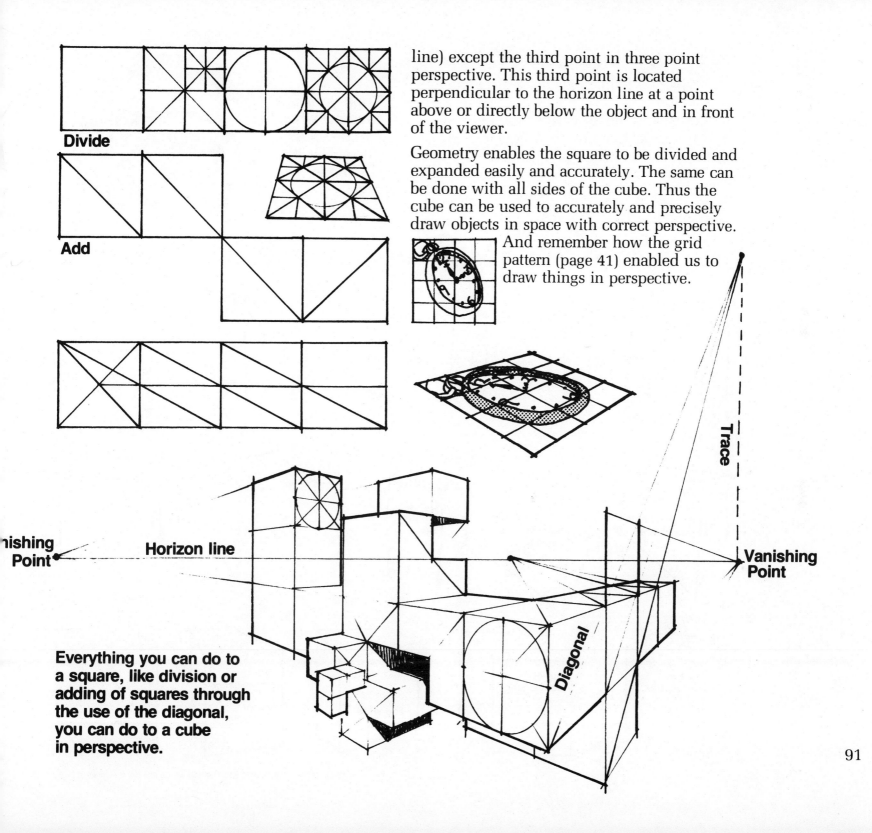

Divide

Add

line) except the third point in three point perspective. This third point is located perpendicular to the horizon line at a point above or directly below the object and in front of the viewer.

Geometry enables the square to be divided and expanded easily and accurately. The same can be done with all sides of the cube. Thus the cube can be used to accurately and precisely draw objects in space with correct perspective. And remember how the grid pattern (page 41) enabled us to draw things in perspective.

Trace

Horizon line

Vanishing Point

Vanishing Point

Diagonal

Everything you can do to a square, like division or adding of squares through the use of the diagonal, you can do to a cube in perspective.

91

Four Rules for Drawing Cubes Freehand

1. Vanishing points must have a common horizon line.
2. The nearest angle must be 90° or greater.
3. All perspective lines converge toward common vanishing points.
4. Accurate proportion is established by eye (intuitive experience).

Train your eye to know when a cube looks correct as it rotates in space.

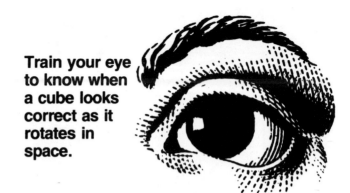

Below a number of cubes have been drawn. Two are correct. The rest contain common drawing errors.

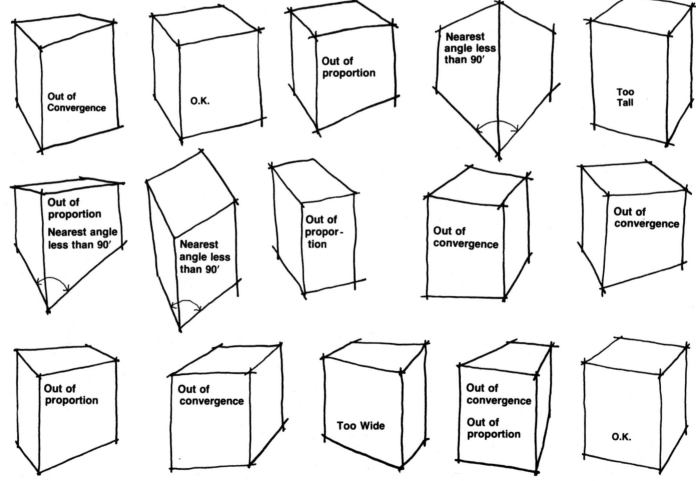

92

Perspective—a new system for designers, Jay Doblin, Whitney Library of Design

The method of using the cube to assist you in drawing requires that you place an outline of the cube over the object to be drawn. You then draw things in relationship to the superimposed cube outline. It is much like copying with a grid pattern.

Use the square as a unit of measurement (one inch or one mile—whatever you need) to be superimposed over the object you want to draw. This unit becomes a measurement grid to draw the object in space.

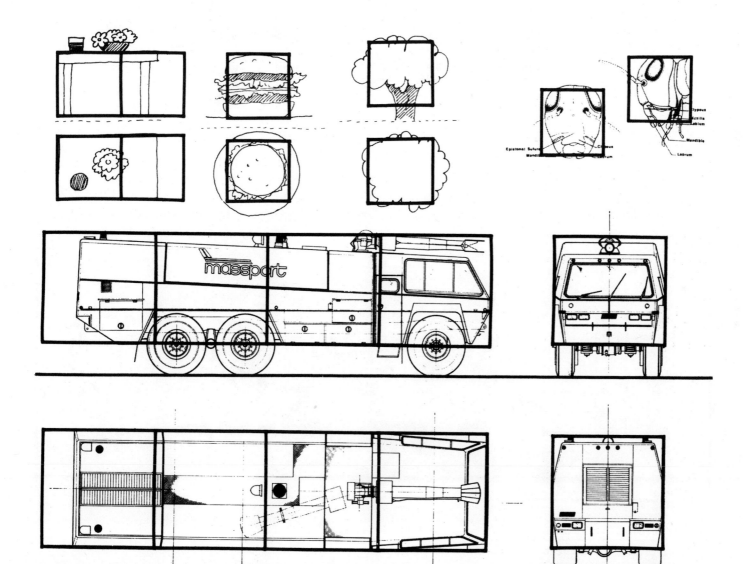

93

Drawings shown here demonstrate the evolution of a drawing using cube-like structures drawn in perspective. The structures are drawn from one vanishing point which is located behind the door. Notice that many of the structures in the room were first drawn very box-like: they are all cubical or three dimensional rectangular boxes.

Concept Design Associates, Salt Lake City, Utah

Use the cube (or divisions of it) as a unit of measurement to develop three dimensional space and the objects within it.

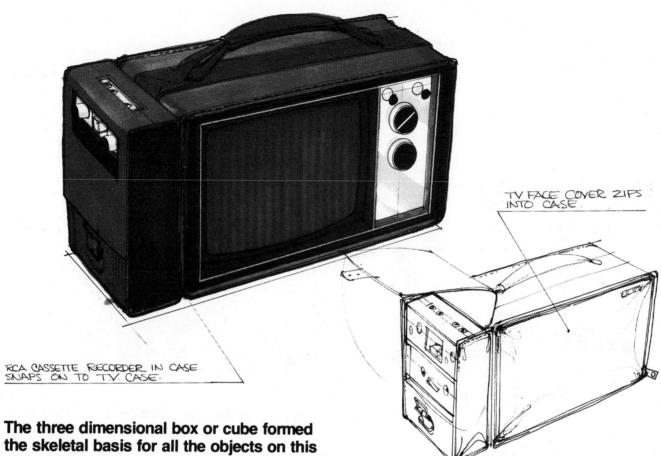

TV FACE COVER ZIPS INTO CASE.

RCA CASSETTE RECORDER IN CASE SNAPS ON TO T.V. CASE.

The three dimensional box or cube formed the skeletal basis for all the objects on this page.

Tucker P. Madawick, division vice president, Industrial Design Department, RCA

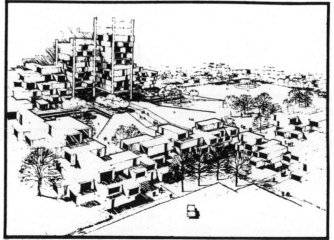

Reprinted by permission, Theodore D. Walker, *Perspective Sketches II,* © 1975. Sketch by Richard Dee, Johnson and Dee, Avon, Conn.

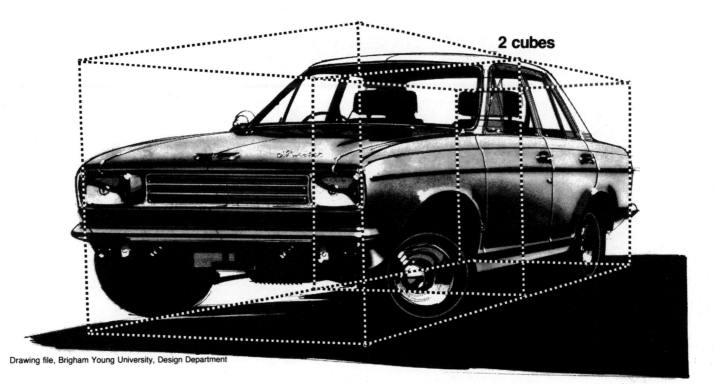

2 cubes

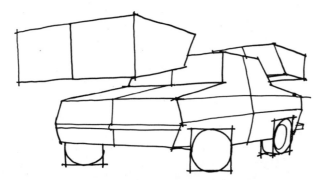

On your paper and through your mind put the car in a large box, then fill it with liquid cement. After it hardens cut away sections of the box revealing the automobile which is inside.

You must see the car within a box and the measurement relationships between the box's side and the surface of the car.

Dotted lines and cut-away portions of this car show how a three dimensional structure assisted in the drawing of the automobile. In this instance, the method of drawing very closely resembles the method probably used for model making. A large block was cut down until the car emerged.

To draw things accurately it is essential to know where all parts of the car would be if drawn—even the parts hidden from view. This enables the object to be accurately drawn in correct perspective.

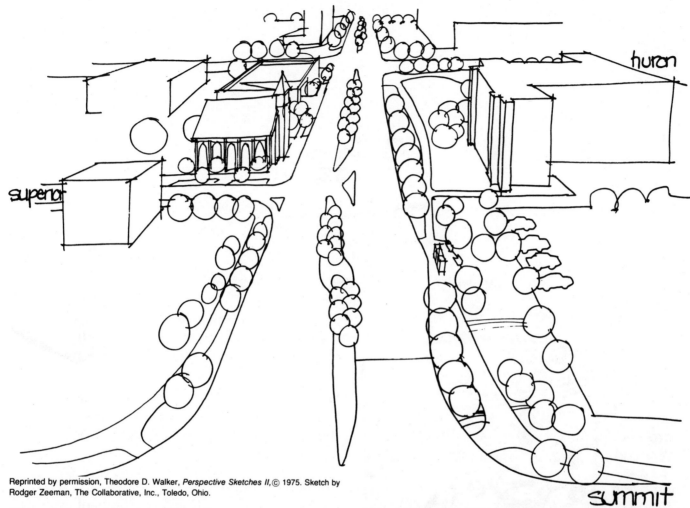

superior

huron

summit

The simple cube can form the drawing basis for nearly all dimensional objects. Picture in your mind's eye any object you may want to draw then put that object into the smallest cube-like box possible. By using the square sides where the object touches as reference points you can construct your sketch. This will work for almost anything from a building to a bug.

Put the things you want to draw in the smallest box possible, then use the box to draw it on your paper.

97

The Ellipse

An ellipse is a circle in perspective.

Ellipse is a technical sounding term for a common element in our lives. An ellipse is an oval shape—what a circle looks like when seen at an angle. An ellipse, in other words, is a circle seen in perspective.

Find an ordinary tin can and see for yourself the relationship of a circle drawn in perspective—an ellipse. As you look straight down on the top of the can you will see a perfectly round circle.

March on down to your nearest store and buy a can of beans, then bring it home where, within the security of your own home, you can study and learn the secrets of the ellipse.

Look down at the top of the can.

David Edwards

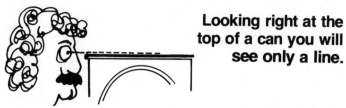

Looking right at the top of a can you will see only a line.

Now take the same can and hold it so that the top is level with your eyes. What you see from this angle is a straight line across the top of the can. Remember it is a circle you are looking at which appears to be a straight line from this angle.

As you lower the can you see more of a circle, but the top does not look exactly round until your eyes are directly over the top of the can looking straight down.

The positions of the can other than straight down make the top look like an elongated circle or an ellipse. These ellipses then are really circles in perspective.

As you rotate the can you will see this.

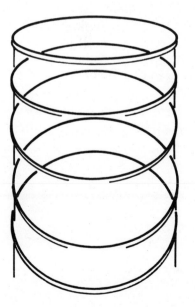

Many things in life have round shapes, but if you will look close you will notice that you see them most often as ellipses or elongated circles.

Take just a minute and list ten items which have circular shapes. Note whether you saw them as true circles or ellipses.

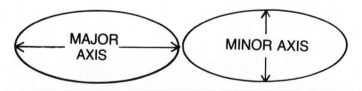
If you are like most people the exercise helped you to realize that you see very few circles, but that most circular shapes are really seen as ellipses.

A circle in perspective is an ellipse or a foreshortened circle.

An ellipse has a major and a minor axis. The major axis is an imaginary line which connects the two widest points of the ellipse. The minor axis connects the two closest points of the ellipse.

MAJOR AXIS   MINOR AXIS

The minor axis is always in the direction of the axle if it is a wheel, the bottle if it is a bottle cap or the shaft if it is a hole.

99

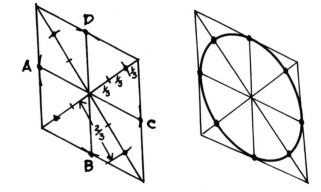

Find or cut a circle out of paper and stick a pin through the middle of the circle. Twist this disk by holding the pin between your fingers and rotating your hand into different angles. You will notice the circle looks like different size ellipses.

David Edwards

If you look close you will also notice that the pin always lines up with the minor axis. If the paper circle were a wheel on your car and the pin were the axle then the axle would always line up with the minor axis of the wheel.

To draw a circle in perspective is very, very simple. First draw an ordinary square with a circle in it which touches all four sides.

Now draw diagonal lines from the corners of the square through the center of the circle. Note that the circle touches the square at A, B, C, and D which are the centers of the sides of the square. Also note that the circle crosses the diagonal lines of the square at points which are 2/3 of the distance from the center of the square to the corner.

First draw a square in perspective. Divide the square into 4 equal quarters by drawing lines connecting the centers of the sides of the square.

Measure ⅔ out on the diagonal from the center to find the line of your circle.

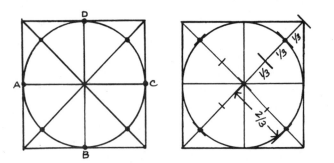

Now draw curved lines from the points of the centers of the sides of the square. When these are all connected you will have drawn a circle in perspective.

Now draw lines from the corners of the square making an X in the center of the square. Where these lines cross is the center of your circle in perspective. You will notice, however, that the center of the square is where the major and minor axes cross. The center of the circle always falls upon the line which forms the minor axis, but it does not fall on the point where the major and minor axes cross.

Go make some skewered disks and look at them in real life to see what we have been talking about!

Look at all the things that you see during the day that you think are flat circles, but are really circles in perspective—ellipses.

You will find many instances when drawing a circle in perspective will be helpful. Some artists even go as far as using a circle as a basis for drawing the way we have used a cube. We recommend a cube-based drawing method because it is much more accurate and versatile. That some artists rely on circles, however, demonstrates how necessary circles are to drawing.

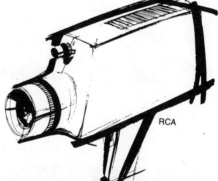

RCA

The minor axis is always in the direction of the axle if it is a wheel, the bottle if it is a bottle cap or the shaft if it is a hole.

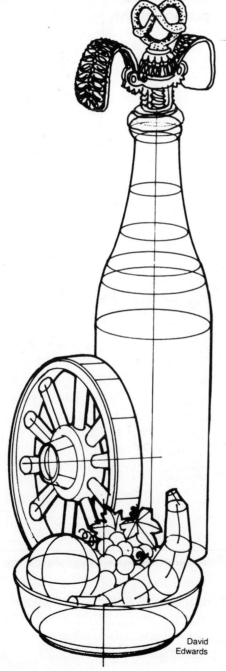

David
Edwards

101

Draw things like you see them, not as you think you see them.

Get a sheet of glass and draw things coming at the glass.

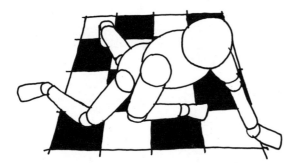

Foreshortening

Foreshortening is the visual appearance that as extensions of objects get close to you they get larger. Also, the connector to that object (the arm, leg, etc.) appears to be very short in relation to the actual size. Notice the objects on this and the following page. The head, hand, foot or whichever portion of the figure is closest to you appears to be larger in size than you would expect it to be for the object shown. And the arm, leg, or neck which connects it to the body appears to be considerably shorter than you would expect.

Foreshortening is nothing more than a combination of the principles of size and perspective as explained on previous pages. An ellipse (a circle in perspective) is a foreshortened circle—an excellent example of foreshortening.

Draw someone throwing a fist at you. You may be surprised to find the fist is about as big as the person throwing it.

Probably the best method for you to use to learn foreshortening would be to trace nature. Place a clear piece of glass in front of you and draw a person with his hand outstretched toward you. Notice how the relative body proportions appear to change. The head is smaller in size than the body. The foot is larger and the leg is hidden from view. The other leg and foot appear small in comparison. The head, body and arms are much larger than the legs. And this man is all feet.

Emphasis

Emphasis is used in drawing to attract attention or dramatize certain portions of a picture.

One black dot in a white field is an example of emphasis. The contrast of the small black area against the white background draws attention to the dot.

A white dot against a black background also creates emphasis. Attention is drawn to the white dot.

The more dots the less emphasis there is. Three dots can emphasize a point, but the more dots the less the degree of contrast and the less effective the emphasis.

Many dots form a pattern of white and black areas which compete with each other. Neither white or black dominates or demands more attention. The more competition for attention the less effective the emphasis.

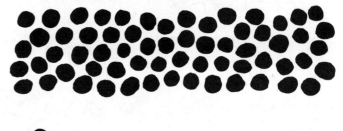

Many different components in a drawing can cause emphasis. Light against dark and color against no color, are forms of emphasis. Detail can cause emphasis when placed in a picture dominated by lack of detail. Change in size in a drawing causes emphasis. Any pattern break will draw attention and thereby emphasize a portion of a drawing. Any unexpected change will create emphasis.

The line below is an example of how emphasis works. Notice that the straight line holds no intrigue at all. However, when a variation in the line occurs your attention is quickly drawn to that variation.

One jog in the line is emphasis. The unexpected variation in the straight line demands your attention.

Two jogs in the line aren't quite as interesting.

The more jogs in the line the less emphasis. When you have a number of jogs in the line as shown here a straight portion would cause emphasis.

The stronger the contrast the better for emphasis. If you want portions of a black and white drawing to stand out, then place them next to the most extreme contrast possible,—black next to white for example. Do the same with color—bright vivid colors against dark drab colors or no color.

You manipulate emphasis! This illustrates white against detail.

Just the opposite is detail against white.

A dot intersecting a line or a dot out of the margin illustrates the impact (or emphasis) when something happens out of context. Emphasis is determined by the inter-relationship (or lack of relationship) of things.

Context is the key to emphasis!

The degree of emphasis caused by any variation in a drawing depends on how it is used within that drawing. For example, a large black dot on a white background will not emphasize any one portion of that drawing. The back dot needs to be small to draw attention to it.

The drawing of the room contains many areas where the principle of emphasis is used to demand attention. The white against the dark creates a direction for the eye to follow as it emphasizes certain portions of the drawing. It is this manipulation of light against dark which is most often used to compose a picture. The artist creates illusion by the contrast and makes the picture hold together by causing your eye to follow a certain direction.

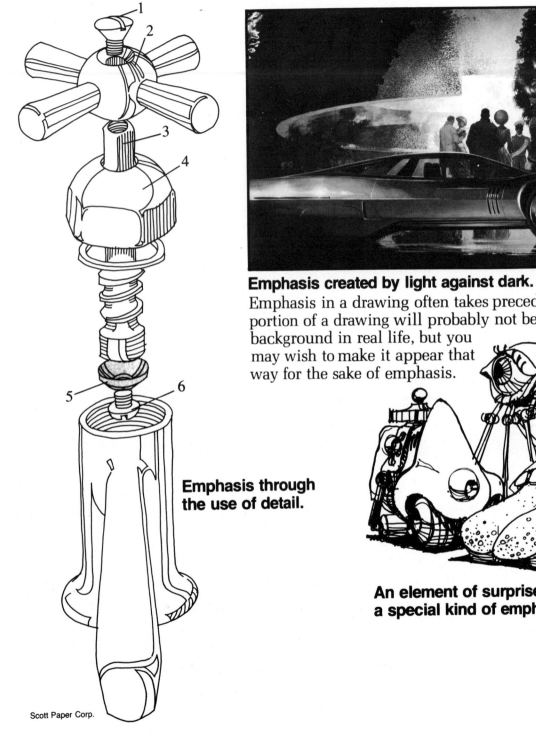

Emphasis through the use of detail.

Emphasis created by light against dark.

Emphasis in a drawing often takes precedent over reality. A portion of a drawing will probably not be white against a black background in real life, but you may wish to make it appear that way for the sake of emphasis.

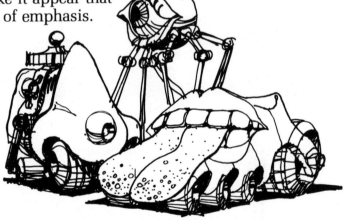

An element of surprise creates a special kind of emphasis.

106

Tremco Inc.

This drawing is very strong. Its stark use of light and dark areas is an example of emphasizing different areas within a drawing.

Employ contrast to a high degree by putting dark areas right next to the light areas.

Concept Design
Associates

Mark Stehrenberger, Illustrator/Designer, La Crescenta, California

108

Pat Mortensen

Be aware of what your eye likes to look at and the path it follows.

Notice the images that your eye picks out. You probably saw the dark areas first on this page. And, if your eye works like most people's eyes work, you looked from left to right. You saw the most emphasized areas first (in this case the dark areas) and you saw things on the top left and moved down or to the right next.

Industrial Design Dept., Sears, Roebuck and Co.

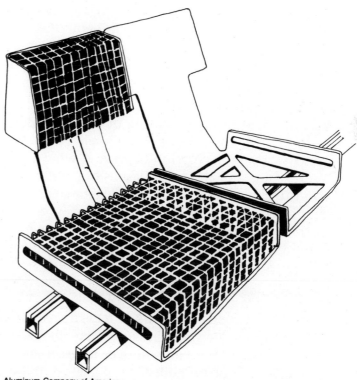

Aluminum Company of America
Corporate Design Division

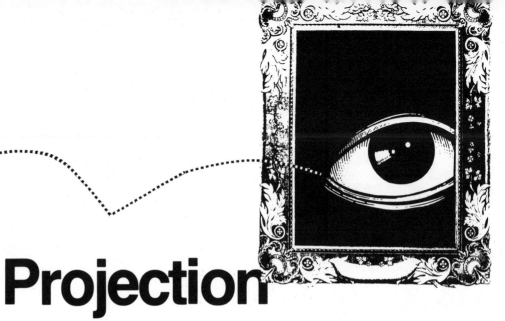

Projection

Put yourself into someone else's shoes—see the drawing from the inside out and the outside in.

Projection is the practice of seeing things not from within, but from many points of view.

Try a mental game which will help communicate to you what projection is. Imagine you are sitting next to yourself. You are an outside observer looking at yourself. You are reading while sitting in a chair. Take a closer look and see inside yourself. See your mind working, trying to understand what you are reading. See the little flashes of energy as you think hard. See your muscles move as you change position. Feel the tenseness as you read something you don't believe. You have many goals, fears, emotions, likes and dislikes which cause you to think in certain ways. Look at some of those goals and emotions. See something you dislike about yourself. Don't be alarmed, everyone has fears or feels dissatisfied with himself. See something you like about yourself. Now look yourself over to learn and understand yourself better.

Hopefully that little exercise helped you see something about yourself from a different viewpoint. What you should learn from it is that everyone has goals, expectations, self images, emotions, and fears that direct his behavior. You see things differently than anyone else. You see things through your eyes, screened by your goals, emotions, knowledge and hangups.

Get into your drawings.
See what they see.
See who views them.

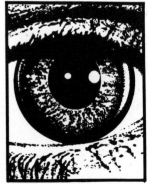

Projection implies that you should attempt, on occasion, to see things not from within, but from another person's viewpoint.

110

Projection is learning to see drawings from the point of view which will give the best solution. There is a saying which goes . . . "What a tiger eats becomes a tiger and what a lion eats becomes a lion." In much the same way, what an artist sees becomes the final drawing. The trick, then, is to see things that will give the best solution to a particular drawing.

Have you ever seen a movie of yourself or heard a tape recording of your voice? You probably didn't sound or act like you thought you did—proof again that you see things in your own unique way.

The following three stories illustrate projection, what it is and how to use it.

Story #1
Once upon a time . . .

. . . and he lived happily ever after.

111

Story #2 Another Point of View

A mother once told an interesting story of how she began to see the world her little children see. She was Christmas shopping with her little boy in New York City. The place was jammed with rushing shoppers. It had been raining, she still had many things to do and her young son was unhappy and complaining. While she was fighting the crowd through an aisle of a store, her son managed to convey to her that his shoe was untied and he was tripping on the lace.

She put her packages on the counter and squatted down to tie his shoe. As she did so, she suddenly saw the picture from his level. He was too small to see the display cases with their colorful items and lights. All he could see were legs, a wet and dirty floor, and big people charging at him from every direction. No wonder he was unhappy; there was nothing interesting or pleasant from his viewpoint.

She picked him up and carried him while she finished her shopping, and quickly headed for home.

Everyone sees the world from a different view and it is essential that you understand other points of view to be able to produce the best drawings.

Put yourself in someone else's shoes.

Story #3 The Tale of the Adventuresome Ant

One day an ant was assigned his first tasks outside the anthill. He was told to drag back a dead grasshopper killed by the elders in a raid the previous day.

Out he went, our young hero. Upon leaving the anthill, he was profoundly impressed and even shocked at the size of the outside world. He had heard tales that the world was larger than his own world, but never had he experienced such massive size.

At once he scurried in search of the grasshopper. As he continued his search, carefully following detailed directions, he came to a barrier that he could not surmount. So he did what any good ant would do; he crawled under.

Upon so doing, he was again confronted with a shock that would have caused a heart attack in any weaker ant. The world was immensely larger than he had dreamed. For it seemed that the anthill had been located under a bushel basket and what he had thought was the outside world was only the area covered by the basket. But now he was faced with the whole world. He realized that he really had been unable to understand his environment until he had gotten out of it. Only now did he see that the anthill was covered by a bushel basket.

He still had not found his grasshopper, so he continued on. Again a barrier stopped him until he was able to burrow under it. And another shock greeted him. For once on the other side of the barrier he realized that the bushel basket was located in a greenhouse and that what he had thought was the big wide world was really only a small greenhouse.

Now that he was outside the greenhouse he could understand.

Well, the story goes on because it turns out that the ant, intelligent as he might be, still hadn't really seen the outside world. For the greenhouse was located just outside center field of the Astrodome in Houston. By the time he had found his grasshopper, he had gained an appreciation of how small his own ant world really was.

Projection suggests eyeballing a particular situation from every conceivable angle. Look at a drawing. See yourself looking at it. See and feel your thoughts and reactions to what you see. Now consider ways of changing it so that you would like what you see better. And look from the inside of the drawing out in much the same way—to see if you could change it to make it better.

Draw a drawing with feeling. As the paper aeroplane suggests in the drawing of the building at the lower right, let yourself float through the room as you draw it. Feel the room and the spaces. Make it all work together.

Don't just draw the space—feel it!

Design Drawing Experiences, William Kirby Lockard, Pepper Publishing

113

Evolution

"Use as many pieces of paper as you need: a new piece for each idea; a new piece each time you want to correct an old idea. Continue until you are satisfied with your drawing!"

R. Arnheim

Many people believe that drawings are done instantly by artists with talent, which is not the case at all. A good drawing is done by someone who understands and practices drawing principles in evolving a drawing from rough to finished stages.

The use of basic shapes to form the skeleton from which a drawing can evolve is an example of drawing evolution.

A drawing often begins as an idea. And often this idea is so abstract that it necessitates locating real objects (or photos of real objects) to use as models to begin the drawing. These models are then interpreted into basic shapes and light and dark areas on a piece of paper. From here a tissue might be overlaid, the original rough idea drawing traced and refined over and over again until a final is reached. This final might then be transferred onto a finished surface for completion and refinement.

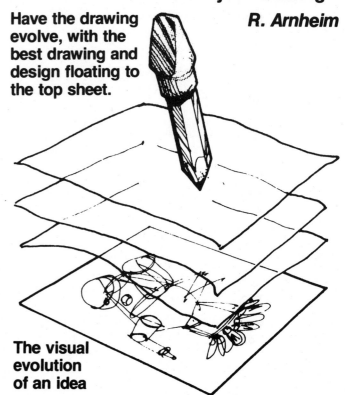

Have the drawing evolve, with the best drawing and design floating to the top sheet.

The visual evolution of an idea

114

THUMBNAILS—small **drawings used to figure out things before you get to the desired end result.**

This same evolutionary method can be used, through drawing to help refine an idea. The drawing solidifies the idea and the drawing evolutionary steps refine it into a good working innovation.

The drawings on this and a few following pages illustrate the evolution of drawings and ideas.

Ah, once   there was a dinosaur,   a pterodactyl,   and some wierd looking

Bob Kurtz & Friends, Standard Oil television commercial

sea creatures and plants. together they... became a layer... of organic material.

And, then with... a little heat, a pool of crude oil, which turned...

Into six tanks of gas, ten thousand ...kilowatts, and a lot more.

Now, we're plumb out pterodactyls, and the like. So when you...
of dinosaurs,

Bob Kurtz & Friends, Standard Oil television commercial

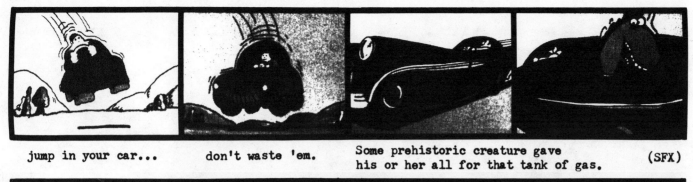

jump in your car...   don't waste 'em.   Some prehistoric creature gave his or her all for that tank of gas.   (SFX)

(Music tag)   (Music tag)   (Music tag)   (Music tag)

Bob Kurtz & Friends, Standard Oil television Commercial

Use a single piece of paper to evolve your idea by lightly sketching your drawing with a pencil; then when you think you've got it do it in pen.

Some of these ideas were developed to very popular finished products. Some were never developed. As drawings evolve they become better or obviously worse. They evolve into useless or useful items.

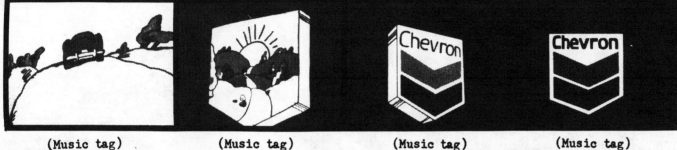

TOOTH BRUSH

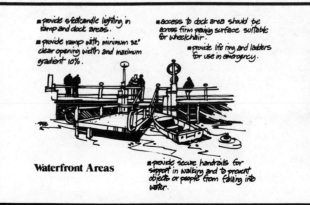

Waterfront Areas

Barrier Free Site Design, Government Publication

117

Work out your drawings as Thumbnail sketches first. Draw the elements, proportions and other needed materials and techniques small before doing it larger.

It's better to work this size and make small mistakes than larger and more finished and make big mistakes

Viewer Completion

If the designer triggers the human imagination and compels the viewer to provide details, he is setting up an ideal learning situation. The artifice of incomplete form leaves room for imagination—the mind then fills in the details and works out the visual form.

Edward A. Hamilton

Roses are Red, violets are _____.

You tried not to say it, but you couldn't help it, could you?

Your mind may be more active than you think. It often fills in details or completes visual images, often without you realizing that it has happened.

Notice how accurately your mind completes the drawings shown here. There is no doubt about what these incomplete lines represent. You know exactly what the drawings portray.

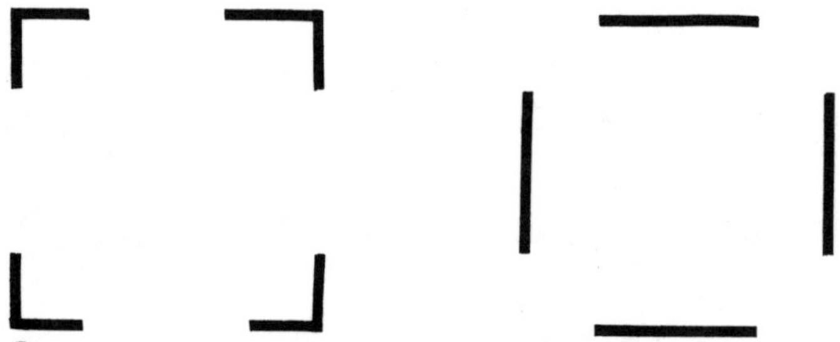

Corners are more important at giving key information than sides.

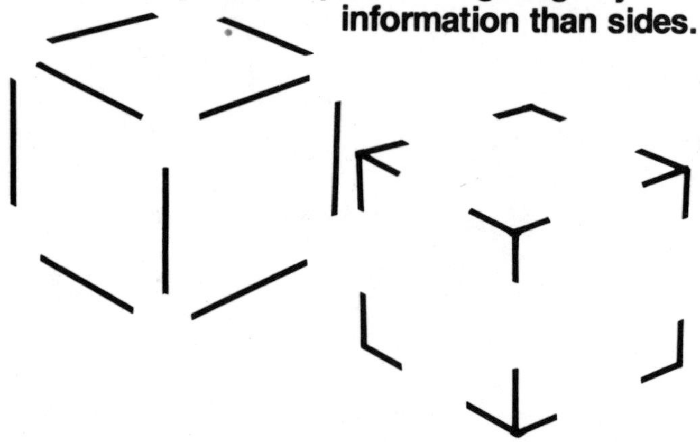

The lines not put into a drawing are as important as those that are.

120

**In drawing . . . the clue to holding the
viewer's attention is to allow him to discover,
and be rewarded in the discovery of
successive levels of visual information.**

W. Lockard

At one stage in its development, each of these
sketches went through a much more completed
form than what you see, but by drawing with
transparent paper overlays and eliminating
unnecessary lines and shapes a "sketchier" look
was achieved to obtain better viewer
involvement in the drawings.

Concept Design Associates
Salt Lake City, Utah

121

Concept Design Associates, Salt Lake City, Utah

Look closely at the drawing. You will be surprised to discover that not a single object is completed. The drawing is composed of fragmented and incomplete parts. What you see is what you want to see. The drawings are made of implied lines, shadows and objects. You mentally add the detail.

122

Drawing file, Brigham Young University, Design Department

Notice how many portions of this automobile are not completed. The car has no fender, roof or back end. Yet you might not have realized this, if you had not been asked to take notice.

It takes practice and skill, but carefully placed implied lines and objects can often say more than accurate detail.

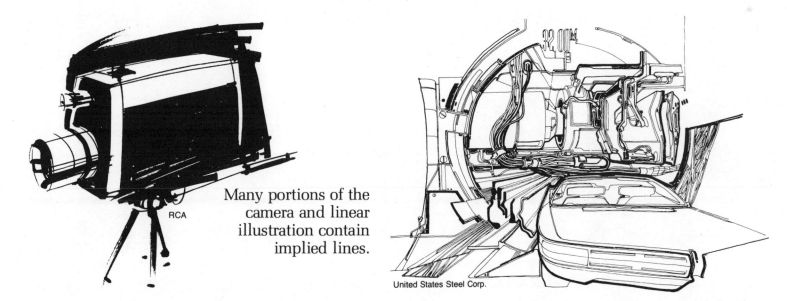

RCA

Many portions of the camera and linear illustration contain implied lines.

United States Steel Corp.

123

Figure Indication

Human figures give scale to drawings and allow viewer involvement.

Human figures are essential to help you understand scale. The trees below would not convey the feeling they do without figures implied below them. And, if you are like many people, you imagine yourself as one of the figures standing below those trees. (See p. 47.)

Notice the size relationships of the things around you.

Dimensions for People Outdoors

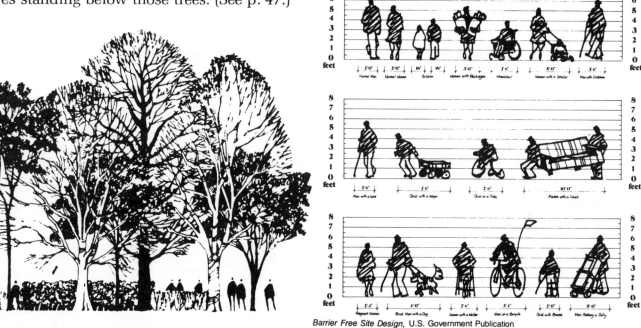

Barrier Free Site Design, U.S. Government Publication

124

**Without the human factor
these drawings would be
less informative.**

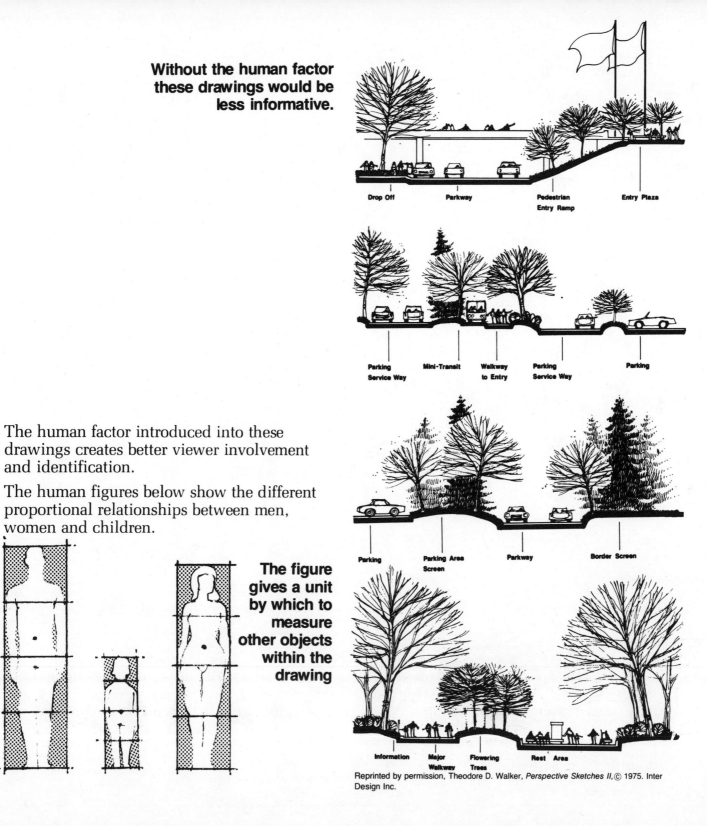

The human factor introduced into these
drawings creates better viewer involvement
and identification.

The human figures below show the different
proportional relationships between men,
women and children.

**The figure
gives a unit
by which to
measure
other objects
within the
drawing**

Drop Off   Parkway   Pedestrian   Entry Plaza
                         Entry Ramp

Parking   Mini-Transit   Walkway   Parking   Parking
Service Way   to Entry   Service Way

Parking   Parking Area   Parkway   Border Screen
             Screen

Information   Major   Flowering   Rest Area
              Walkway   Trees

Reprinted by permission, Theodore D. Walker, *Perspective Sketches II,* © 1975. Inter
Design Inc.

125

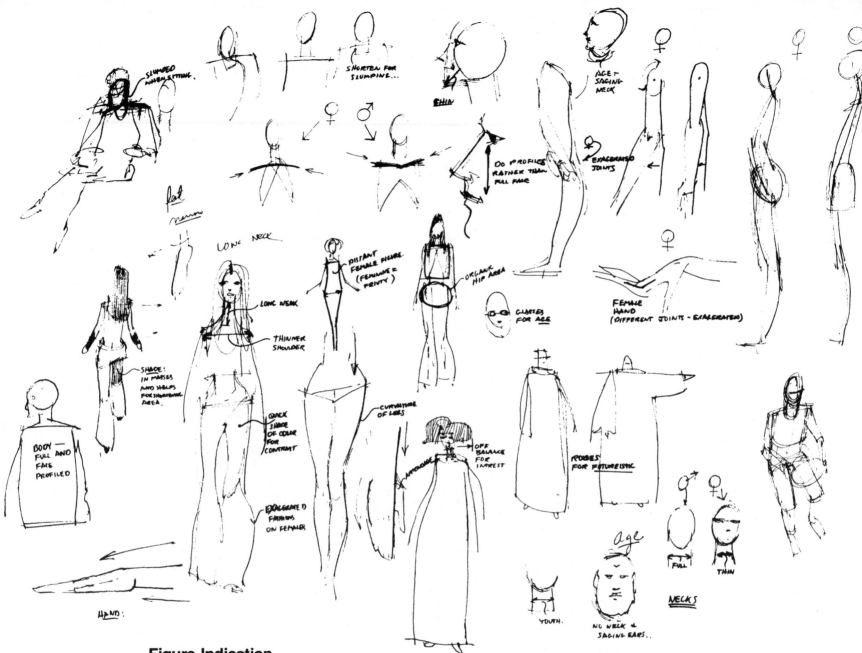

Figure Indication

The drawings on these two pages show how to draw quick sketchy human figures. It is these kinds of figure drawings that suggest the presence of human beings in architectural renderings.

You would usually use this type of figure in a drawing where other things are most important (such as the building in an architectural rendering) but where the indicated presence of humans strengthens the drawing.

126

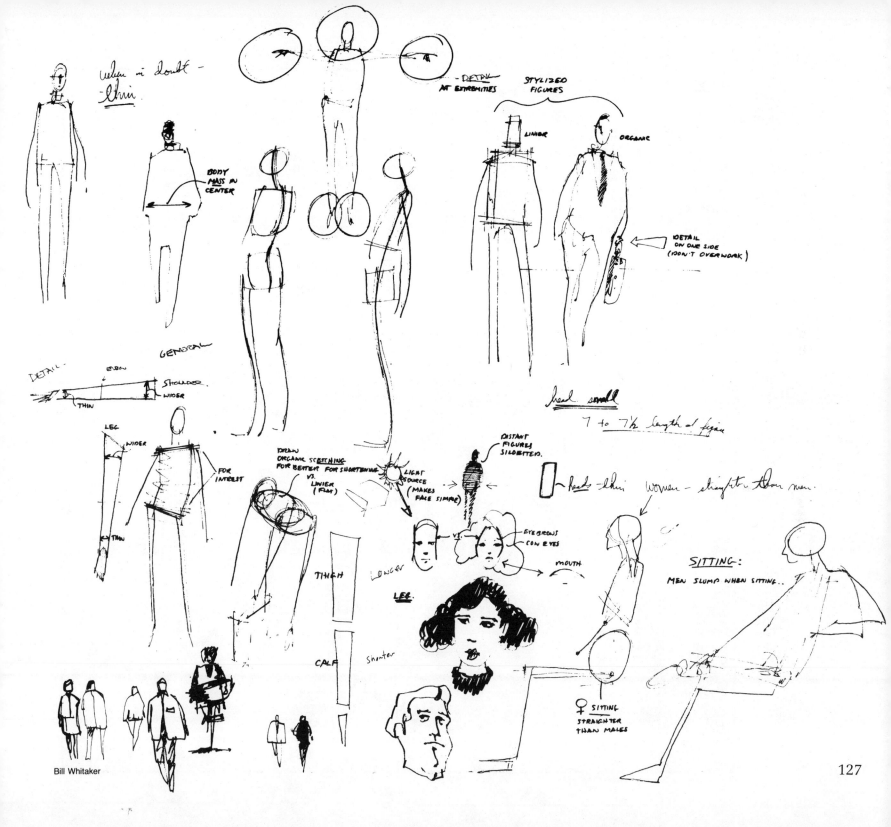

when in doubt - thin

BODY MASS IN CENTER

- DETAIL AT EXTREMITIES

STYLIZED FIGURES

LINIER   ORGANIC

DETAIL ON ONE SIDE (DON'T OVERWORK)

DETAIL   GENERAL   ELBOW   SHOULDER   WIDER   THIN

head small

7 to 7½ length of figure

LEG   WIDER   THIN

FOR INTEREST

DRAW ORGANIC SKETCHING FOR BETTER FOR SHORTENING VS. LINIER (FLAT)

LIGHT SOURCE (MAKES FACE SIMPLE)

DISTANT FIGURES SILHOUETTED

head - thin   women - straighter than men

THIGH   LONGER   VS.   EYEBROWS   LOW EYES   MOUTH

LEG

CALF   Shorter

SITTING:
MEN SLUMP WHEN SITTING.

♀ SITTING STRAIGHTER THAN MALES

Bill Whitaker

127

Ken Dallison, illustrator, Toyota Motor Sales, U.S.A.

Art Center College, Honnold, Reibsamen & Rex, Los Angeles, California

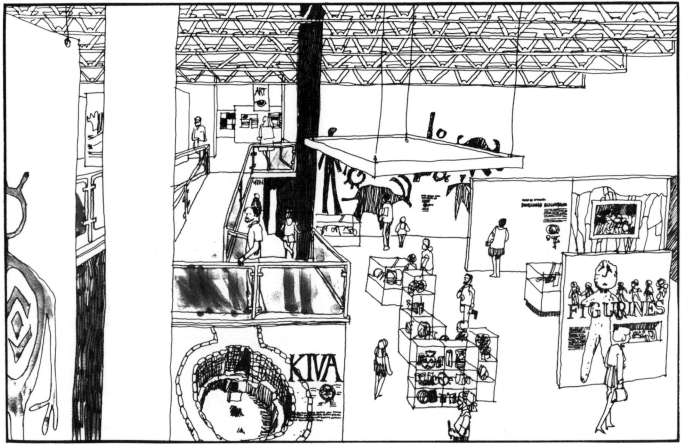

Concept Design Associates, Salt Lake City, Utah

People looking at a drawing identify with people in a drawing.

We know what people look like, their sizes and shapes especially, because we are people ourselves. When objects are placed next to people, the people act as a scale to give a true sense of size to the unfamiliar objects.

Exterior Design in Architecture, Y. Ashihara, ©1972 Litton Educational Publishing, Inc.
Reprinted by permission of Van Nostrand Reinhold Co.

Goobers

The wholeness of the drawing exceeds the sum of all its parts.

If a basketball player misses a basket he doesn't quit—he tries again. If a mathematician miscalculates a math problem he doesn't give up—he tries again. If you trip and fall you don't lie down and cry—you get up and try again. But for some strange reason, when most people try to draw for the first time, if it isn't perfect they give up.

Mistakes are a fact of life. Everybody makes mistakes in every field of endeavor. And drawing is no different. A mistake is no big deal. It certainly isn't grounds for quitting.

Different people have different drawing techniques. You may like someone else's style better than your own. And he may like your style better than his. But in the end it is all the same. It is the act of transferring images from inside our mind onto a surface where others can share them. We may not all be Rembrandts, but we can all benefit from the ability to transform abstract mental images into real objects for communication and evaluation.

Mistakes must be an accepted part of the drawing processes. They should not be the biggest barrier to success, but instead, one of the great helps to improvement. What we do wrong teaches us what to do right—it isn't proof of failure.

It is better to have tried and blown it than to have never tried at all.

Ima Success

You made a mistake. Big deal! That's why they put these things on the ends of pencils.

E. Ray Serr

130

Sketch Book

Make doodling, drawing and sketching a natural part of your life's activities.

Throughout life we are taught to carry note-books. The process begins in school and continues into our home and work. Why not make a portion of our notebooks (our notes to ourselves and others) visual? Make them sketchbooks.

Try a few experiments and see if they work.

1. Put visual sketches with your school notes. It will make the notes more interesting to read and more difficult to forget.

2. Introduce a visual element into the notes to yourself. Then try to forget those notes.

3. Include visual sketches into your attempts to understand things. This will introduce a holistic and relational mental process with your logical and analytical mind. It will give you new problem solution insights.

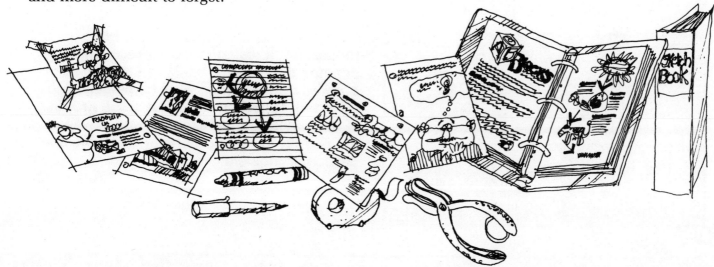

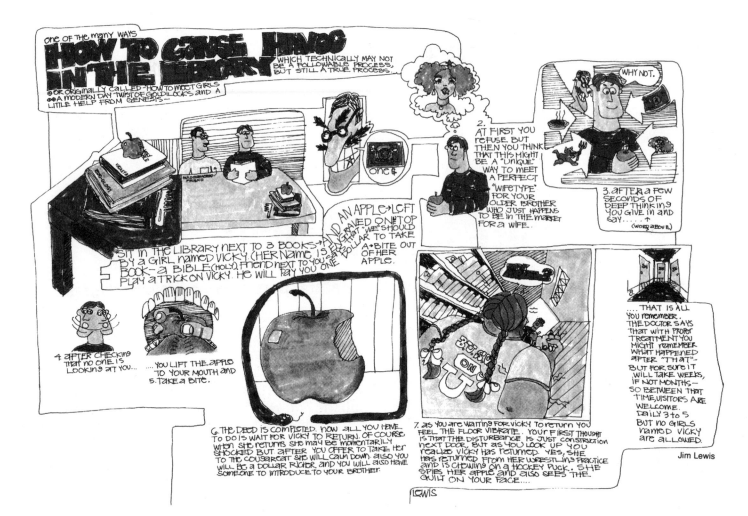

One of the many ways

HOW TO CAUSE HAVOC IN THE LIBRARY

WHICH TECHNICALLY MAY NOT BE A FOLLOWABLE PROCESS, BUT STILL A TRUE PROCESS...

⊕ OR ORIGINALLY CALLED "HOW TO MEET GIRLS.
⊕⊕ A MODERN DAY TWIST OF GOLDILOCKS AND A LITTLE HELP FROM GENESIS—

WHY NOT.

2. AT FIRST YOU REFUSE. BUT THEN YOU THINK THAT THIS MIGHT BE A "UNIQUE" WAY TO MEET A PERFECT "WIFE TYPE" FOR YOUR OLDER BROTHER WHO JUST HAPPENS TO BE IN THE MARKET FOR A WIFE.

3. AFTER A FEW SECONDS OF DEEP THINKING YOU GIVE IN AND SAY..... ↑ (WORD ABOVE)

1. SIT IN THE LIBRARY NEXT TO 3 BOOKS → AND AN APPLE ← LEFT BY A GIRL NAMED VICKY (HER NAME IS ENGRAVED ON → TOP BOOK — A BIBLE (HOLY) FRIEND NEXT TO YOU SAYS DOLLAR TO TAKE PLAY A TRICK ON VICKY. HE WILL PAY YOU ONE A → BITE OUT OF HER APPLE.

4. AFTER CHECKING THAT NO ONE IS LOOKING AT YOU....

.... YOU LIFT THE APPLE TO YOUR MOUTH AND 5. TAKE A BITE.

6. THE DEED IS COMPLETED. NOW ALL YOU HAVE TO DO IS WAIT FOR VICKY TO RETURN. OF COURSE WHEN SHE RETURNS SHE MAY BE MOMENTARILY SHOCKED BUT AFTER YOU OFFER TO TAKE HER TO THE COUGARETT SHE WILL CALM DOWN. ALSO YOU WILL BE A DOLLAR RICHER AND YOU WILL ALSO HAVE SOMEONE TO INTRODUCE TO YOUR BROTHER.

7. AS YOU ARE WAITING FOR VICKY TO RETURN YOU FEEL THE FLOOR VIBRATE. YOUR FIRST THOUGHT IS THAT THE DISTURBANCE IS JUST CONSTRUCTION NEXT DOOR, BUT AS YOU LOOK UP YOU REALIZE VICKY HAS RETURNED. YES, SHE HAS RETURNED FROM HER WRESTLING PRACTICE AND IS CHEWING ON A HOCKEY PUCK. SHE SPIES HER APPLE AND ALSO SEES THE GUILT ON YOUR FACE....

.... THAT IS ALL YOU REMEMBER. THE DOCTOR SAYS THAT WITH PROPER TREATMENT YOU MIGHT REMEMBER WHAT HAPPENED AFTER "THAT"— BUT FOR SURE IT WILL TAKE WEEKS, IF NOT MONTHS— SO BETWEEN THAT TIME, VISITORS ARE WELCOME. DAILY 3 TO 5 BUT NO GIRLS NAMED VICKY ARE ALLOWED.

Jim Lewis

LEWIS

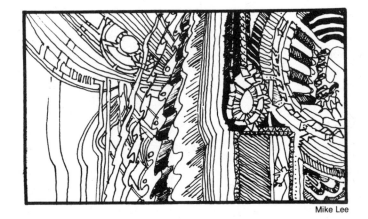

Mike Lee

Drawing is not simply a gesture, but a moderator, a visual thought process which enables the artist to transform into an ordered consequence what he perceives in visionary experience. For the artist, drawing is actually a form of experiencing, a way of measuring the proportions of existence at a particular moment.

Edward Hill

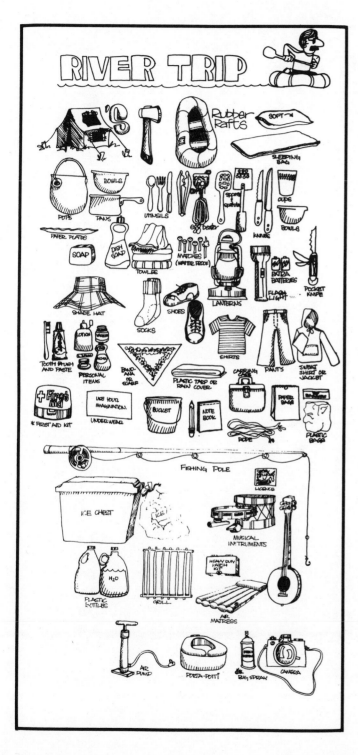

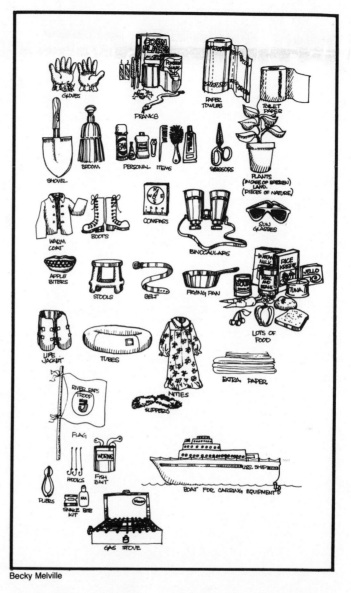

Becky Melville

Doodles and visual exercises will expand your creativity and drawing ability. These visual images were done by college students as an assignment. Notice the new and different look to what might be termed useless information. In verbal language these drawings could be a boring waste.

Your eye has the final say

No matter the techniques
or methods used, the final
say as to whether or not
the drawing works is the
eye. If it looks right it
works, if it looks wrong it
doesn't work!

LUMINOUS PAINT

Make Your Watches, Clocks, Etc., Visible by Night

The very latest discovery in the scientific world. Hitherto, practically unobtainable except at an exorbitant price, we have at last succeeded in producing this remarkable LUMINOUS PAINT, which, applied to the surface of any article, emits rays of white light, rendering it perfectly visible in the dark. THE DARKER THE NIGHT, THE MORE BRILLIANT IT SHINES. Quite simple to use. Anyone—you can do it. A little applied to the dial of your watch or clock will enable you to tell the time by night. You can coat the push buttons or switch plates of your electric lights, match boxes, and innumerable other articles; make your own Luminous Crucifixes, Luminous Rosaries, etc. Bottle containing sufficient to coat several small articles, Price 25c. Larger sizes 50c and $1 postpaid. Johnson Smith & Co., Dept. 502 Racine, Wis.

Microphone Transmitter Button

$1.00 POST-PAID

You can easily make a highly sensitive detectophone by using this Transmitter Button to collect the sound waves. You can build your own outfit without buying expensive equipment. It is simple and inexpensive. You can install an outfit in your home and hear conversations being held all over the house. You can connect up different rooms of a hotel. This outfit was used by secret service operatives during the war. It is being used on the stage. It is ultra-sensitive and is the greatest invention in micro-phones. You can mount the button almost anywhere—card board boxes, stove pipes, stiff calendars, on the wall behind a picture frame, etc. Button is so light and small it cannot be detected. Persons can be overheard without suspecting it. You can listen in on conversations in another room. A deaf person in the audience can hear the speaker. Connected to phonograph, piano or other musical instrument, music can be heard hundreds of feet away. Button may be used to renew telephone transmitters; often makes an old line "talk-up" when nothing else will. The ideal microphone for radio use; carries heavy current and is extremely sensitive. Amplifies radio signals. Countless other similar uses will suggest themselves. Experimenters find the Button useful for hundreds of experiments along the lines of telephones, amplifiers, loud speakers, etc. Many fascinating stunts may be devised, such as holding the button against the throat or chest to reproduce speech without sound waves. $5.00 is given to anyone who sends in a new suggestion for the use of the Button providing the manufacturers find it suitable for use in their literature. PRICE $1.00 POSTPAID ANYWHERE.

JOHNSON SMITH & CO., Dept. 502 Racine, Wis.

U. S. BABY TANK

25 Cents

It goes with real Yankee Pep—by its own power

Most remarkable Toy ever invented. By drawing the Tank backward, either with the hand or over the floor or table and then placing it down, it will crawl along, overcoming all obstacles, in the same lifelike manner as the larger Tank that proved so deadly in the great war. What makes it go is somewhat of a mystery, for there is no mechanism to wind up as is usually understood with mechanical toys, yet this tank will keep plodding along ten times longer than the ordinary run of toys. It will perform dozens of the most wonderful stunts; it will go backward or forward at will. 2½ inches long. Price only 25 cents prepaid.

ANARCHIST BOMBS

One of these glass vials dropped in a room full of people will cause more consternation than a limburger cheese. The smell entirely disappears in a short time. 10c a Box, 3 Boxes for 25c

INVISIBLE INK

The most confidential messages can be written with this Ink, for the writing MAKES NO MARK. Cannot be seen unless you know the secret. Invaluable for many reasons. Keep your postals and other private memorandums away from prying eyes. Great fun for playing practical jokes. Only 15c Bottle

MIDGET BIBLE

GREAT CURIOSITY

Smallest Bible in the world. Size of a postage stamp. 200 Pages. Said to bring good luck to the owner. A genuine work of art. Must be seen to be appreciated. Make good money selling them to friends, church acquaintances, etc. PRICE 15c each, 3 for 40c, 12 for $1.35, 100 for $7.50. Also obtainable in Leather Binding, with gold edges. Price 50c each, 3 for $1.25, $4.50 per doz. Magnifying Glass for use with Midget Bible, 15c.

Every Boy His Own Toy Maker

Greatest boys' book written. Tells how to make a Pinhole Camera, a Canoe, model Railroads, a Telephone, Boomerang, Telegraph Instrument, Box Kite, etc. $1.00 postpaid.

Surprise Matches

More fun than fighting with your wife. Look just like ordinary matches. 10c

---

STAGE MONEY

With a bunch of these bills it is easy for each person of limited means to appear prosperous by flashing a roll of these bills at the proper time and peeling off a genuine bill or two from the outside of the roll, the effect created will be found to be all that can be desired. Prices, postpaid: 40 Bills 20c, 125 for 50c, or $3.50 thousand postpaid.

Wonderful X-Ray Tube

10c

A wonderful little Instrument producing optical illusions both surprising and startling. With it you can see what is apparently the bones of your fingers, the lead in a lead pencil, the interior opening in a pipe stem, and many other similar illusions. A mystery that no one has been able to satisfactorily explain. Price 10c, 3 for 25c, 1 dozen 75c. Johnson Smith & Co.

Good Luck Ring

Quaint and Novel Design

A VERY striking and uncommon ring. Silver finish, skull and crossbone design, with two brilliant, flashing gems sparkling out of the eyes. Said by many to bring Good Luck to the wearer, hence its name, Good Luck Ring. Very unique ring that you will take a pride in wearing. ONLY 25 CENTS.

Exploding Cigarettes

JUST LIKE ORDINARY CIGARETTES, BUT SUCH REAL STARTLERS! The box contains ten genuine cigarettes of excellent quality. They appear so real, but when each cigarette is about one-third smoked, the victim gets a very great surprise as it goes off with a loud BANG! A great mirth provoker yet entirely harmless. Price 25c per box.

Popular Watch Charms

15c

ONLY 3 for 40c; $1.35 doz.

Very pretty little curiosities and decidedly novel. Fitted with Magnifying Lenses that enlarge the pictures to a very surprising degree; in fact, it seems almost incredible that a clear picture could be possible in such a small compass, and how sharp and distinct they show up when you look through. Come in assorted views—Actresses, Views of Panama Canal, Lord's Prayer in type, etc.

CIGARETTE MAKER

Roll your own and save money. Makes them better and quicker besides saving more than half. Use your favorite brand of tobacco. Neat, useful and handy. Pocket size, weighs ½ oz. Made entirely of metal, nickel-plated. Price 25c postpaid.

BLANK CARTRIDGE PISTOL

Price $1.00 Postpaid

This well made and effective Pistol is modelled on the pattern of the latest type of Revolver, the appearance of which alone is enough to scare a burglar, whilst, when loaded, it will probably prove just as effective as a revolver with real bullets, without the danger to life. It takes the standard .22 Calibre Blank Cartridges, that are obtainable most everywhere. Even the most timid women can use it with perfect safety and frighten a thief without risk to herself or anyone else. A Great Protection Against Burglars, Tramps and Dogs. You can have it lying about without the danger attached to other revolvers. We sell large numbers around the 4th of July. Well made of solid Metal. PRICE ONLY $1.00 Postpaid. Blank Cartridges 22-cal. shipped by express only, 50c per 100. Johnson Smith & Co., Dept. 502 Racine, Wis.

Sneezing Powder

Place a very small amount of this powder on the back of your hand and blow it into the air, and everyone in the room or car will begin to sneeze without knowing the reason why. It is most amusing to hear their remarks, as they never suspect the real source, but think they have caught it one from the other. Between the laughing and sneezing you yourself will be having the time of your life. For parties, political meetings, car rides, or any place at all where there is a gathering of people, it is the greatest joke out. Price 10c or 3 for 25c

Mystic Skeleton

10c pd.

A jointed figure of a skeleton 14 in. in height, will dance to music and perform various gyrations and movements while the operator may be some distance from it.

Serpent's Eggs

Box contains 12 eggs. When lit with a match, each one gradually hatches itself into a snake several feet long, which curls and twists about in a most lifelike manner. Price per box 10c ppd.

BOYS! BOYS! BOYS!

THROW YOUR VOICE

Into a trunk, under the bed or anywhere. Lots of fun fooling the teacher, policeman or friends.

THE VENTRILO

a little instrument, fits in the mouth out of sight, used with above for Bird Calls, etc. Anyone can use it.

Never Fails. A 32-page book on ventriloquism, and the Ventrilo, ALL FOR 10c postpaid.

ITCHING POWDER

This is another good practical joke; the intense discomfiture of your victims to everyone but themselves is thoroughly enjoyable. All that is necessary to start the ball rolling is to deposit a little of the powder on a person's hand and the powder can be relied upon to do the rest. The result is a vigorous scratch, then some more scratch, and still some more. 10c box, 3 boxes for 25c or 75c per doz boxes postpaid.

Great Fire Eater

Most Sensational Trick of the Day!

With the Fire Eater in his possession any person can become a perfect salamander, apparently breathing fire and ejecting thousands of brilliant sparks from his mouth, to the horror and consternation of all beholders. Harmless fun for all times, seasons and places. If you wish to produce a decided sensation in your neighborhood don't fail to procure one. We send the Fire Eater with all the materials, in a handsome box, the cover of which is highly ornamented with illustrations in various colors. Price 35c

SQUIRT ROSE

25c

A REAL STARTLER. This is the most popular of all squirt tricks. The flower in your coat looks so fresh and sweet that everyone is tempted to inhale the delightful perfume. Then is the moment to press the bulb. Geewhillikens! Don't they jump?

LOOK

Rapid Visualization

Visual thinking is experienced to the fullest when seeing, imagining and drawing merge into active interplay.

Robert McKim

Rapid visualization is the creative, imaginative use of drawing to the fullest degree. It is seeing and creating all rolled into one. Rapid visualization is the expansion of the mind expressed in real form.

To get a better idea of how rapid visualization works, study the ads on the previous page. Let the pictures help your mind's eye dream about what the ads mean to you. Picture yourself with the gadgets as you did when you were younger. Handle the items, use them, make them work for you—all in your mind's eye.

Develop the mind's eye.

Rapid visualization is a physical representation of the images which shift about in our mind's eye. By drawing these fleeting images we can gain time for evaluation and refinement.

As you think of something, a picture often comes to mind. And you have probably noticed that those mental images seem to be very sketchy. You may think that you see something in detail, but as you begin to draw you find vague areas. Rapid visualization allows refinement and detailed understanding of the cloudy images.

Or you may encounter visual images that are in exact detail. The life of those fleeting thoughts is so short, however, that a physical record of what the mind conceived is important.

137

Do more than draw the car. Walk around it, touch it and drive it with your pencil.

This car is an example of rapid visualization in that it was drawn rapidly using felt tip pens. The drawing is very well done considering the quick medium used for rapid results.

Drawing file, Brigham Young University, Design Department

In either instance, if you take time to worry about the quality of the drawing, then the thought can quickly be lost. Rapid visualization is just that—a quick drawing, a spontaneous record.

A designer uses rapid visualization to understand how a car looks and feels before it is built. He can know every intimate part of the car and its operation before it ever is manufactured.

Drawing usually means careful study and an artistic reproduction of an object that is seen. Rapid visualization would be a quick interpretation of that object as our mind conceives it.

As depicted on the next page, a botanist uses rapid visualization to better understand the parts and functions of a plant. Through it he also conveys to others the concepts he knows.

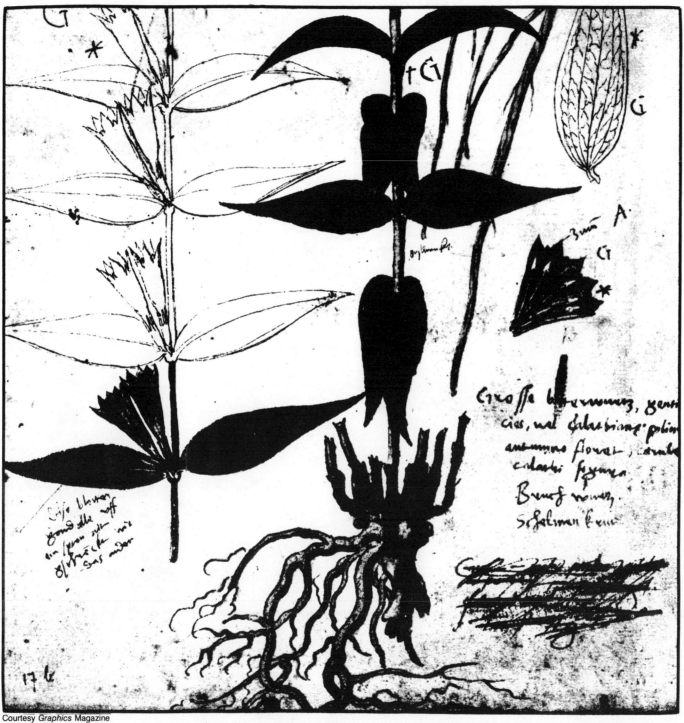

139

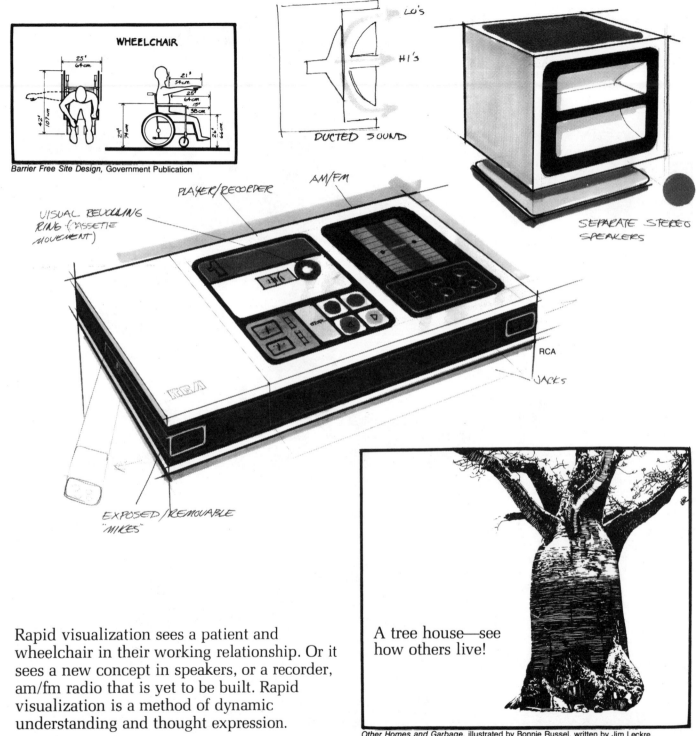

WHEELCHAIR

25'
64cm

21'
54cm

25'
64cm

15'
38cm

42'
107cm

21'
74cm

24'
66cm

Barrier Free Site Design, Government Publication

LO'S

HI'S

DUCTED SOUND

SEPARATE STEREO
SPEAKERS

VISUAL REVOLVING
RING (CASSETTE
MOVEMENT)

PLAYER/RECORDER

AM/FM

RCA

RCA

JACKS

EXPOSED/REMOVABLE
"MIKES"

Rapid visualization sees a patient and
wheelchair in their working relationship. Or it
sees a new concept in speakers, or a recorder,
am/fm radio that is yet to be built. Rapid
visualization is a method of dynamic
understanding and thought expression.

140

A tree house—see
how others live!

Other Homes and Garbage, illustrated by Bonnie Russel, written by Jim Leckre,
Gil Masters, Harry Whitehouse, Lily Young. ©1975 Sierra Club Books

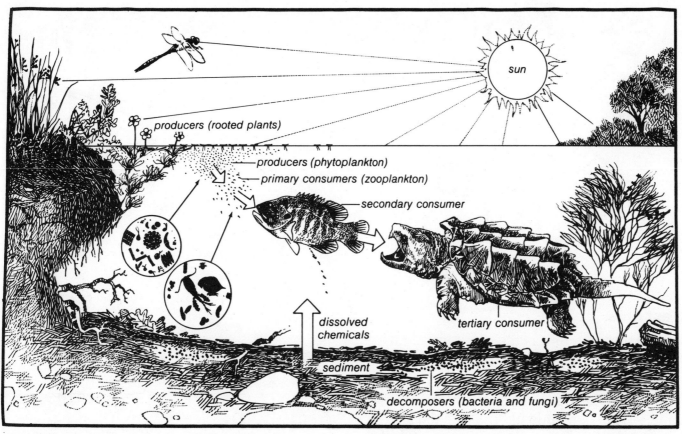

Living in the Environment, "Concepts, Problems and Alternatives," G. Tyler Miller, Jr., Wadsworth Publishing Co.

producers (rooted plants)

sun

producers (phytoplankton)

primary consumers (zooplankton)

secondary consumer

tertiary consumer

dissolved chemicals

sediment

decomposers (bacteria and fungi)

With relatively few words we are able to understand a fresh water ecosystem through the use of visualization and words. It would take many pages of text to even closely convey the complete and complicated message that one drawing can do. The drawing shows a complicated interrelationship that words alone could not convey.

141

Kirk Henrichsen

Fast Draw

Rapid visualization is the quick visual expression of a fleeting instance. It is drawing put to work.

Let's consider the analogy of a baseball pitcher. As he winds up to throw the ball he must subconsciously consider speed, wind direction, distance, spin on the ball, trajectory and many other essentials which allow him to throw a strike. When he first practiced to become a baseball pitcher it was necessary for him to consciously consider all these elements before each pitch. With practice, however, throwing the ball became more automatic and more easily controlled.

Drawing relates to rapid visualization as throwing a baseball does to pitching. Rapid visualization is the subconscious use of drawing to accomplish the goal. It is drawing without thinking about drawing itself. It is drawing done in a quick and natural way and then evaluated later as a finished product.

142

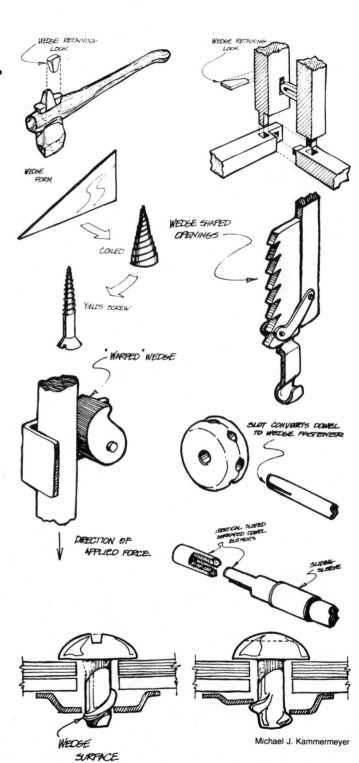

Michael J. Kammermeyer

Scott Bevan

Rapid Visualization is the method for dynamic understanding and thought expression.

The graphic language should stress three qualities
1. Selective Emphasis
2. Originality
3. Economy

Cream together 1 8 oz pkg cream cheese and 2 cub margarine

Blend in 3 c. flour and ¾ tsp salt

Roll out to ½ inch thick

Cut into 1 by 3 inch strips

Make a groove and fill with jam or jelly

Bake on cookie sheet 15-20 min at 350°

Carol Wade

144

Rapid visualization is a physical representation of the images which shift about in our mind's eye. By drawing these fleeting images we can gain time for evaluation and refinement.

As you think of something a picture often comes to mind. And you have probably noticed that those mental images seemed to be very sketchy. You may think that you see something in detail, but as you begin to draw you find vague areas. Rapid visualization allows refinement and detailed understanding of the cloudy images.

Or you may encounter visual images that are in exact detail. The life of those fleeting thoughts is so short however, that a physical record, a drawing of what the mind conceived, is important.

In either instance, if you take time to worry about the quality of the drawing, then the thought can quickly be lost. Rapid visualization is just that—a quick drawing, a spontaneous record.

Cut your drawing time down. Do what you need to produce the quality of drawing necessary for the individual situation.

Quickly finish your drawing. Judge the work when it is finished, not while it is being done.

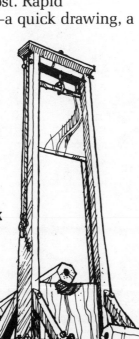

This book portrays in visual and verbal terms the concept of visualization—drawing used as a tool for Ideation, Understanding and Communication.

Drawing, as explained in the book, is not always an end in itself. Drawing is often used as a tool for Ideation (thinking), Notation (understanding) and Communication (transfer of messages).

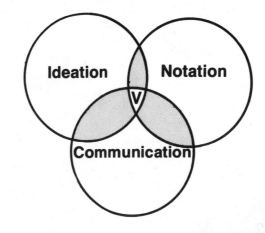

V = Visualization

The overlapping circles, which represent the main areas of drawing used as a tool or mental process, form a small triangular shape in the center which signifies rapid visualization. And rapid visualization is drawing, depending on the situation, done as quickly as possible to achieve the desired result. This form of drawing might be likened to a household tool. When you fix a leaky faucet, for instance, you don't continue holding the wrench, you use it as a tool to finish the job, then you put it down. Rapid visualization is a tool.

It is dynamic. It is applied drawing rather than drawing for art purposes. It is "quick, useful and to-the-point."

Ideation

"A drawing acts as the reflection of the visual mind. On its surface we can probe, test, and develop the workings of our peculiar vision."

Edward Hill

Ideation is the process of getting and refining good ideas. This section of the book shows how drawing helps get and refine good ideas.

Most ideas are illusive creatures. They usually begin as mental images—foggy and incomplete. Ideas need refining, detail, evaluation and expansion.

Drawing enables the solidifying of ideas. It is an interim step between the thought and emergence of an idea. After the spark of creative thought, drawing is the step where the thought can be expanded and evaluated.

Since ideas and mental images are foggy, fleeting and incomplete, it is imperative that they be captured and studied. Drawing is one way this can be done. Drawing allows you to bring the idea to life. It allows you to change, judge and evaluate your thoughts. Drawing provides you the opportunity to see if your seedling thought will grow into a weed or a flower. Some of the most beautiful flowers begin as ugly sprouts—and the ugliest weeds look like innocent plants as they pop through the earth. Plants must grow so that their true potential can be recognized. Just as growth helps a new plant to mature, drawing helps an idea to mature.

Drawing helps develop ideas worth communicating

Ideation is visual thinking on paper.

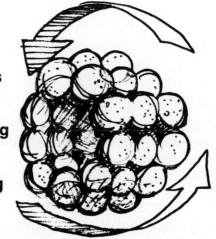

147

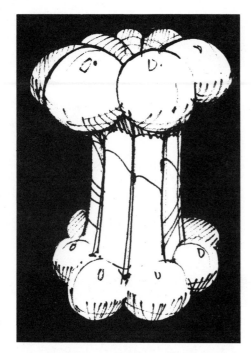

**Establish
visual
metaphors**

**See your
ideas
to test
your ideas**

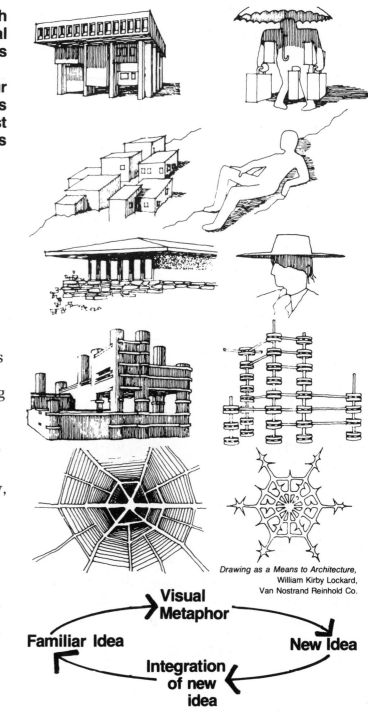

*Drawing as a Means to Architecture,
William Kirby Lockard,
Van Nostrand Reinhold Co.*

To understand the way that drawing solidifies ideas, it is important to remember that the drawing is analogous to the idea. The drawing is not the idea, but it is a graphic representation of what the idea is like. It is a visual representation of what may come to be.

If you look at the process in reverse you can see the relationship. A drawing is NOT reality, it is a representation of what reality means to you. A drawing is an abstraction of reality.

**——— This is like that ———
——— That is like this ———**

Illustrations shown here are visual metaphors. They are mental exercises to help you understand the "IS LIKE" drawing thought process. Look at each and try to understand how they relate. How the building "IS LIKE" the man with the umbrella; how the spider web "IS LIKE" the snowflake; etc.

148

Paul Coker, *Mad Magazine*, E.C. Publications

DOGMA

BOONDOGGLE

COMBAT

DYNAMITE

RAMROD

NAVIGATOR

Drawing is an "IS LIKE" tool. Drawing is what an idea "IS LIKE" or what reality "IS LIKE." It is not an idea or reality but simply represents what each "IS LIKE."

The illustrations here are visual abstractions of verbal thoughts. Notice how the drawings say—in a very different way—what the words are. Can you think of other word visualizations?

The next two pages are what one person saw when he was asked to visually expand an arrow. Try a similar exercise centered around almost any word you desire. Some things might seem corny, but you'll find it a fun way to learn how drawing, ideation and visualization are inter-related.

The visualization of a mental process shown here is how Lawrence Halprin, a well-known landscape architect, solves his design problems.

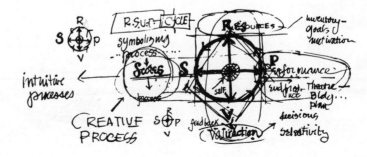

Lawrence Halprin

149

ARROWS

PIERCED ARROW

AERONAUT.

NO

ARROGANT

ARROWHE

LIGHTER THAN AIR

Mark Shultz
Carl Haynie
Kirk Henrichsen
Becky Melville

SCHOOL OF ARROWS

ARROW NAUTICAL.

ARROW PARFESIAN

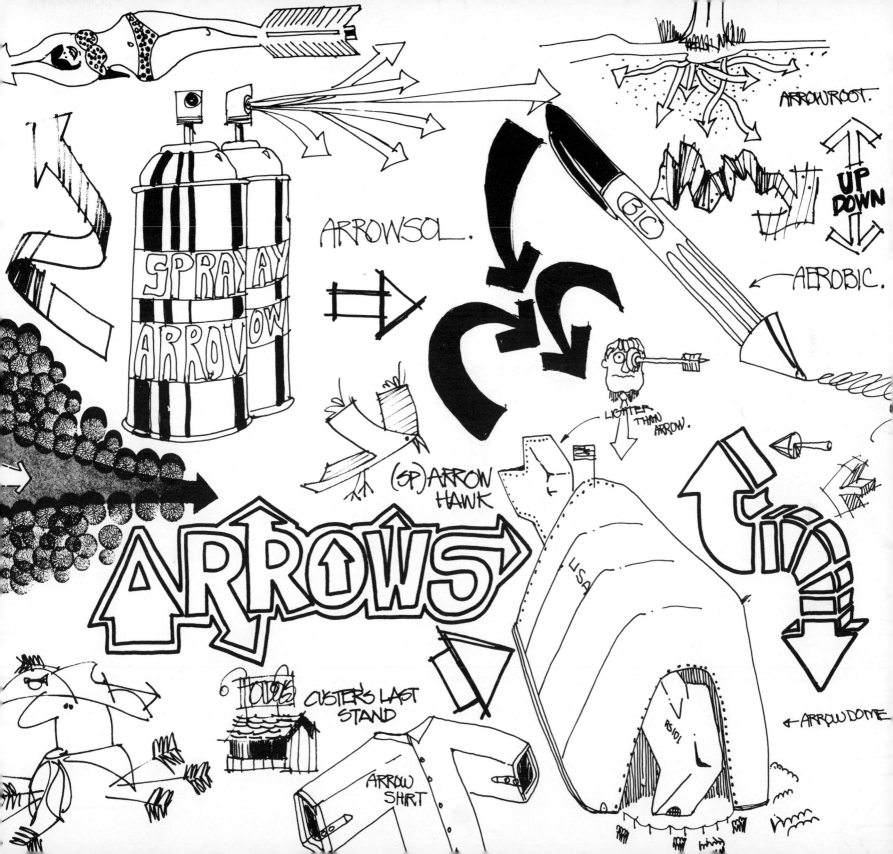

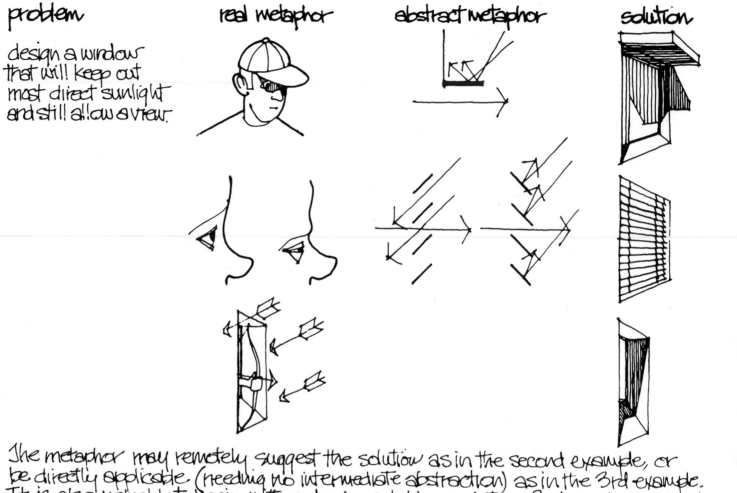

problem | real metaphor | abstract metaphor | solution

design a window
that will keep out
most direct sunlight
and still allow a view.

The metaphor may remotely suggest the solution as in the second example, or be directly applicable (needing no intermediate abstraction) as in the 3rd example. It is also valuable to begin with a design solution and then find a visual metaphor to explain it.

Design Drawing Experiences, William Kirby Lockard, Pepper Publishing

A problem solver will sometimes use a visual metaphor in finding the solution to a problem. He will compare an actual situation or thing to an abstract visual idea. This process combines seemingly unrelated thoughts into new relationships and thinking directions. Though some of the visual solutions may seem ridiculous, when you can finally see the connection it will be logical and make sense.

The clue to holding the viewer's attention is to allow him to discover, and be rewarded in the discovery, successive levels of visual information.

William Kirby Lockard

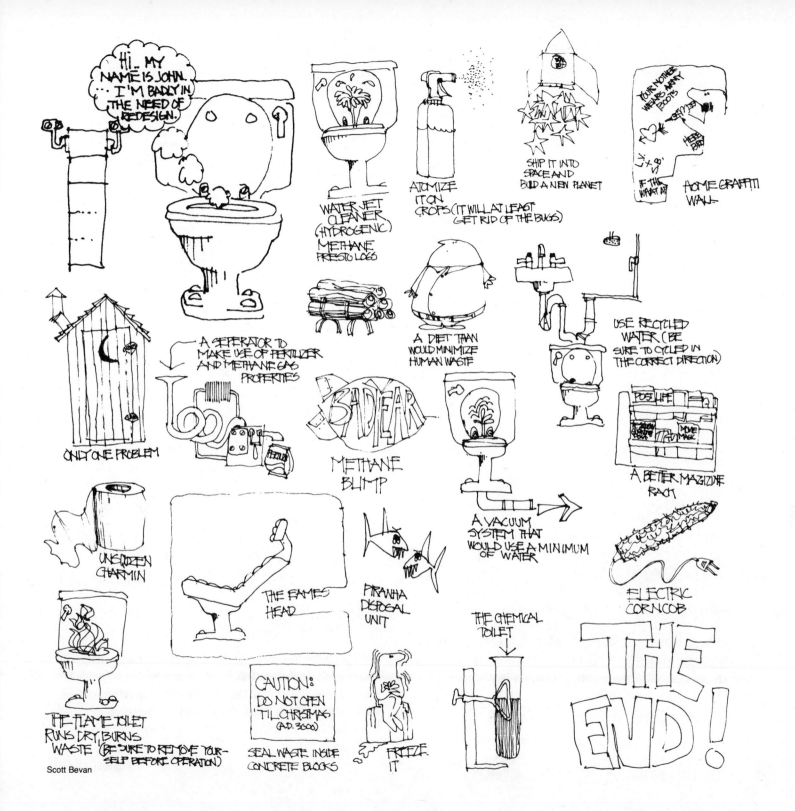

Scott Bevan

153

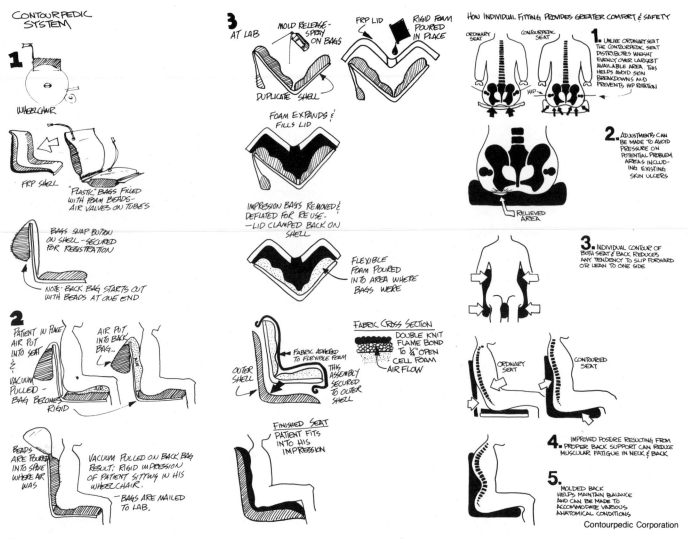

CONTOURPEDIC SYSTEM

1
WHEELCHAIR
FRP SHELL
"PLASTIC" BAGS FILLED WITH FOAM BEADS—AIR VALVES ON TUBES

BAGS SNAP BUTTON ON SHELL—SECURED FOR REGISTRATION

NOTE—BACK BAG STARTS OUT WITH BEADS AT ONE END

2
PATIENT IN PLACE AIR PUT INTO SEAT & VACUUM PULLED—BAG BECOMES RIGID
AIR PUT INTO BACK BAG...

BEADS ARE POURED INTO SPACE WHERE AIR WAS
VACUUM PULLED ON BACK BAG RESULT: RIGID IMPRESSION OF PATIENT SITTING IN HIS WHEELCHAIR.
—BAGS ARE MAILED TO LAB.

3 AT LAB
MOLD RELEASE—SPRAY ON BAGS
FRP LID
RIGID FOAM POURED IN PLACE
DUPLICATE SHELL

FOAM EXPANDS & FILLS LID

IMPRESSION BAGS REMOVED & DEFLATED FOR RE USE.—LID CLAMPED BACK ON SHELL

FLEXIBLE FOAM POURED INTO AREA WHERE BAGS WERE

FABRIC CROSS SECTION
DOUBLE KNIT FLAME BOND TO ¼" OPEN CELL FOAM AIR FLOW

OUTER SHELL
FABRIC ADHERED TO FLEXIBLE FOAM THIS ASSEMBLY SECURED TO OUTER SHELL

FINISHED SEAT PATIENT FITS INTO HIS IMPRESSION

HOW INDIVIDUAL FITTING PROVIDES GREATER COMFORT & SAFETY

ORDINARY SEAT   CONTOURPEDIC SEAT

1. UNLIKE ORDINARY SEAT THE CONTOURPEDIC SEAT DISTRIBUTES WEIGHT EVENLY OVER LARGEST AVAILABLE AREA. THIS HELPS AVOID SKIN BREAKDOWNS AND PREVENTS HIP ROTATION

HIP

2. ADJUSTMENTS CAN BE MADE TO AVOID PRESSURE ON POTENTIAL PROBLEM AREAS INCLUDING EXISTING SKIN ULCERS

RELIEVED AREA

3. INDIVIDUAL CONTOUR OF BOTH SEAT & BACK REDUCES ANY TENDENCY TO SLIP FORWARD OR LEAN TO ONE SIDE

ORDINARY SEAT   CONTOURED SEAT

4. IMPROVED POSTURE RESULTING FROM PROPER BACK SUPPORT CAN REDUCE MUSCULAR FATIGUE IN NECK & BACK

5. MOLDED BACK HELPS MAINTAIN BALANCE AND CAN BE MADE TO ACCOMMODATE VARIOUS ANATOMICAL CONDITIONS

Contourpedic Corporation

The sketches here communicate how a wheel chair can be custom-designed. The problem is spacial in nature and so lends itself to visual representation. And by visually analyzing the problem, the solution becomes obvious and more easily solved.

The next page is a visual solution to a communication problem.

Language allows us to communicate and express; but before that, it clarifies, connects, and forms thought. Drawing does the same. The first function of both is precommunicate: to sharpen perception, to clarify it, and to give it an ordered form.
Edward Hill

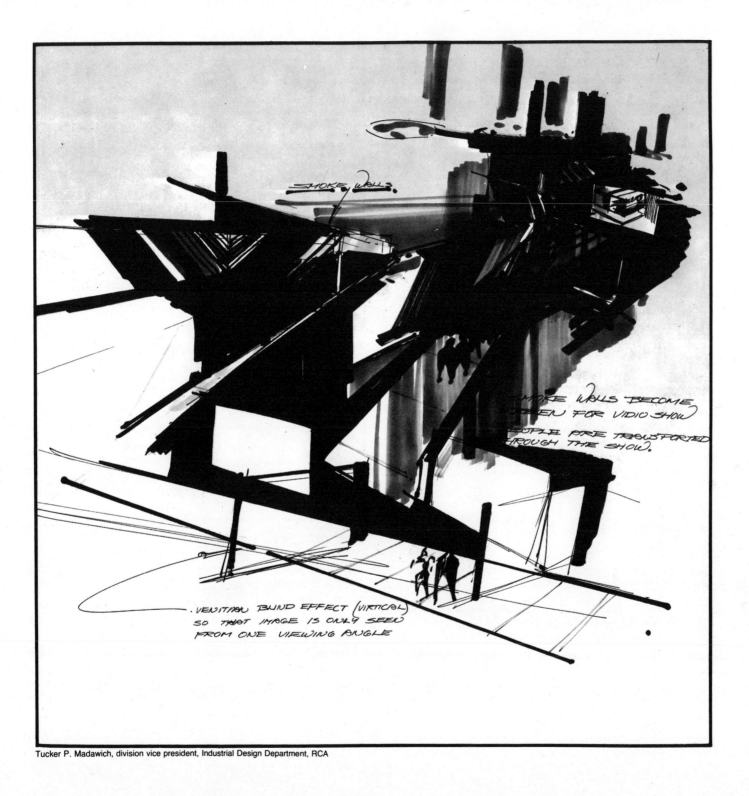

SMOKE WALLS.

SMOKE WALLS BECOME
SCREEN FOR VIDIO SHOW
PEOPLE ARE TRANSPORTED
THROUGH THE SHOW.

. VENITIAN BLIND EFFECT (VIRTICAL)
. SO THAT IMAGE IS ONLY SEEN
FROM ONE VIEWING ANGLE

155

Tucker P. Madawich, division vice president, Industrial Design Department, RCA

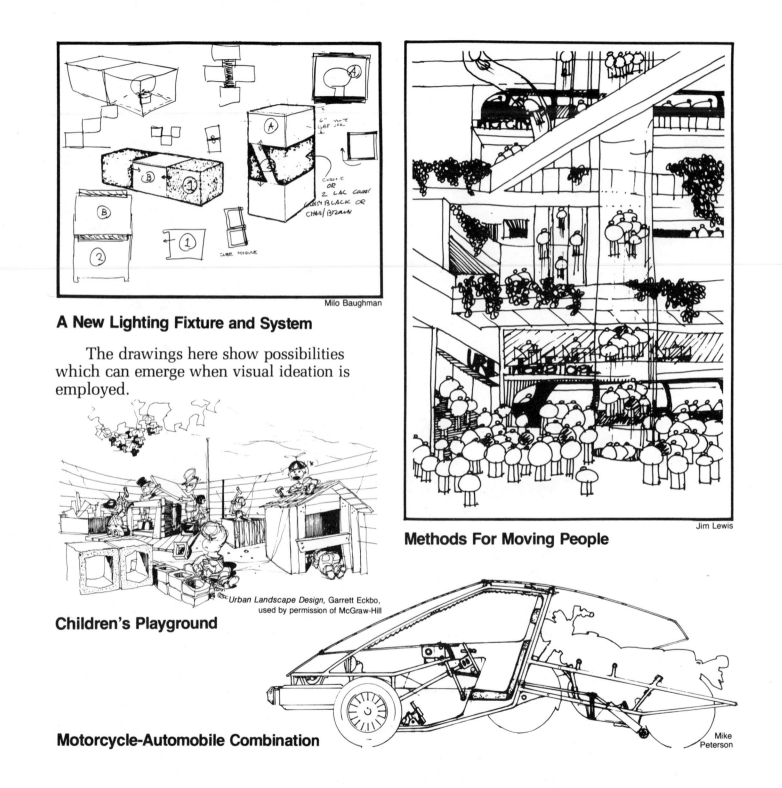

Milo Baughman

A New Lighting Fixture and System

The drawings here show possibilities which can emerge when visual ideation is employed.

Urban Landscape Design, Garrett Eckbo, used by permission of McGraw-Hill

Children's Playground

Jim Lewis

Methods For Moving People

Mike Peterson

Motorcycle-Automobile Combination

156

By Robert McCall

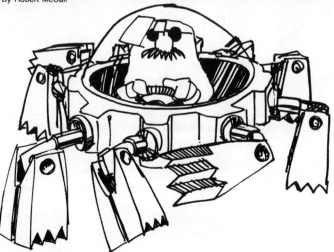

Visual representation of ideas allows for judgment of a near reality. Seeing what something "will be like" before it happens allows you to make rational improvements. You are able to judge after it has emerged from the idea stage into the created stage, but before it is built. You can see what the future holds before it gets here.

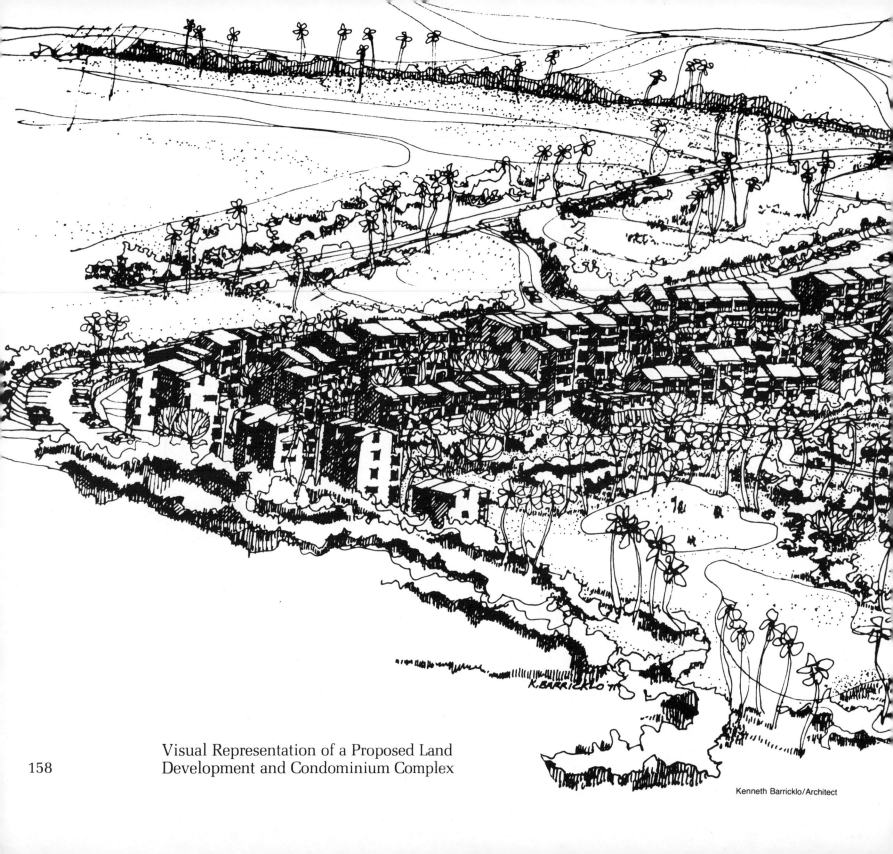

158   Visual Representation of a Proposed Land
Development and Condominium Complex

Kenneth Barricklo/Architect

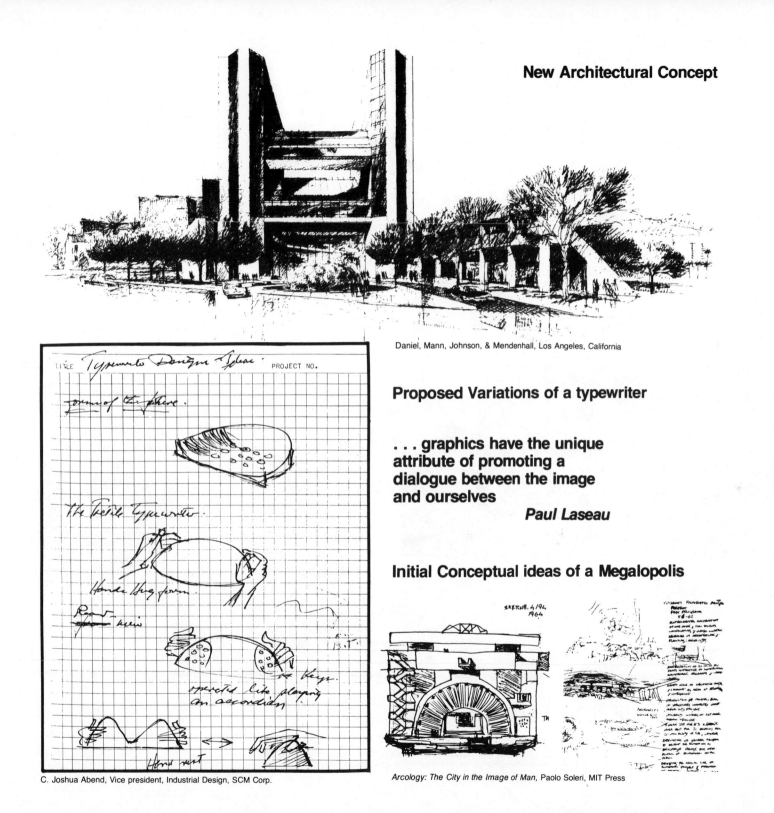

New Architectural Concept

Daniel, Mann, Johnson, & Mendenhall, Los Angeles, California

Proposed Variations of a typewriter

**. . . graphics have the unique
attribute of promoting a
dialogue between the image
and ourselves**
Paul Laseau

Initial Conceptual ideas of a Megalopolis

C. Joshua Abend, Vice president, Industrial Design, SCM Corp.

Arcology: The City in the Image of Man, Paolo Soleri, MIT Press

159

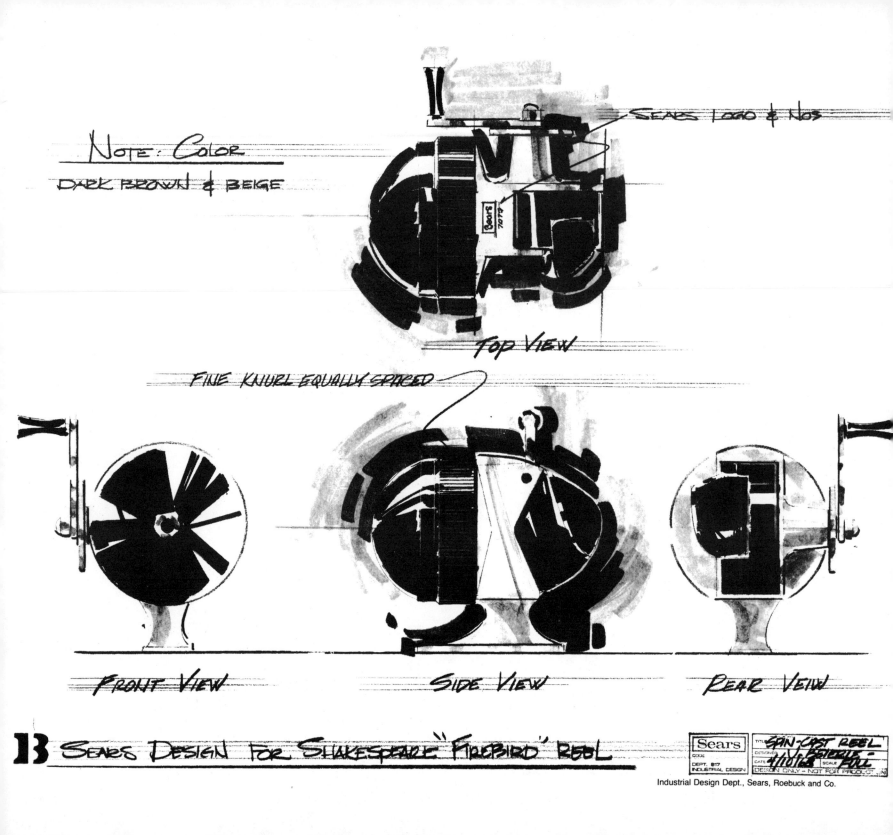

NOTE: COLOR
DARK BROWN & BEIGE

SEARS LOGO & NOS

TOP VIEW

FINE KNURL EQUALLY SPACED

FRONT VIEW

SIDE VIEW

REAR VEIW

13 SEARS DESIGN FOR SHAKESPEARE "FIREBIRD" REEL

Sears
DEPT. 817
INDUSTRIAL DESIGN

TITLE SPIN-CAST REEL
DESIGNER J. BELLMAN
DATE 4/10/68   SCALE FULL
DESIGN ONLY – NOT FOR PRODUCTION

Industrial Design Dept., Sears, Roebuck and Co.

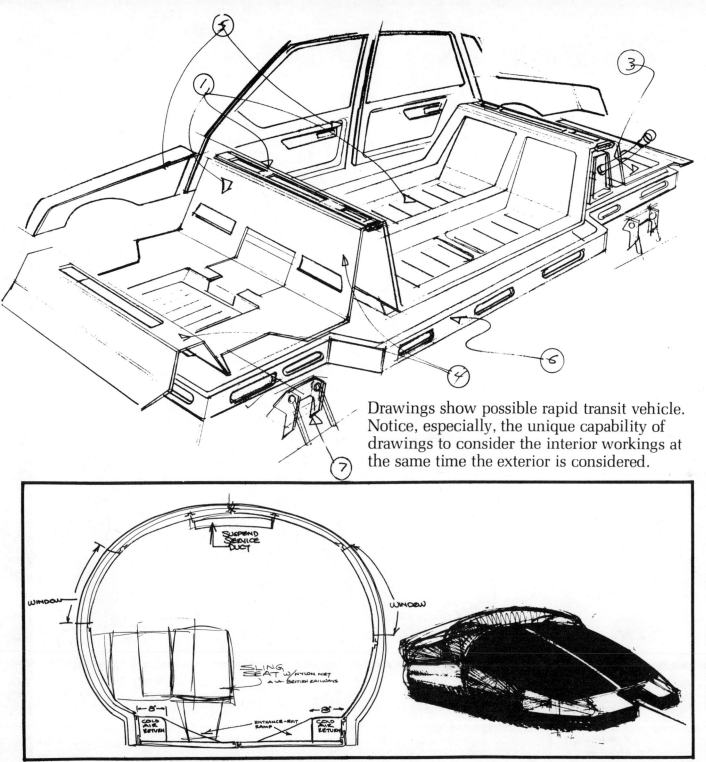

Drawings show possible rapid transit vehicle. Notice, especially, the unique capability of drawings to consider the interior workings at the same time the exterior is considered.

SUSPEND SERVICE DUCT

WINDOW

WINDOW

SLING SEAT w/ NYLON NET à la BRITISH RAILWAYS

8'

8'

COLD AIR RETURN

COLD AIR RETURN

ENTRANCE-EXIT RAMP

Aluminum Company of America, Corporate Design Division

161

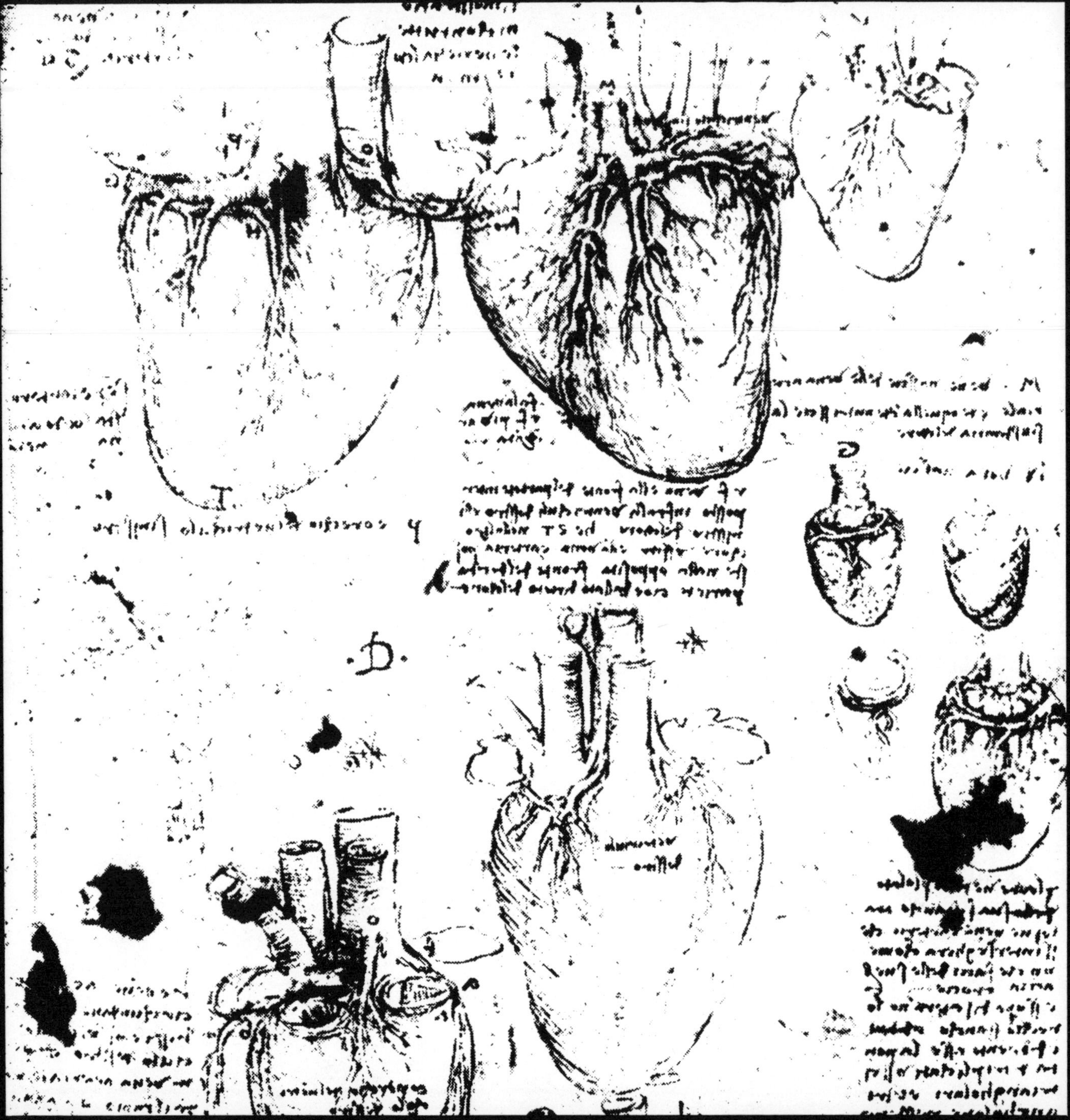

Notation

Leonardo da Vinci's anatomical drawings are so remarkably successful not only because he had the artistic ability to draw what he saw but because he saw every part of the human body as a contraption designed by a fellow inventor. He saw every muscle, bone, or tendon as shaped for its purpose and representative of a tool.

Rudolf Arnheim

Notation is the concept that drawing is a great teacher and an aid to remembering.

Leonardo da Vinci used drawing to help him remember and understand the anatomy of the human body. Drawing was a valuable tool of learning, understanding and remembering to da Vinci.

Notice the drawing which depicts how to start a fire by friction. As you look at the illustration, it becomes obvious that the artist must have known how to start a fire by friction. He certainly knew the importance of all elements in the drawing. He had to understand what he was drawing in order to be able to draw it accurately.

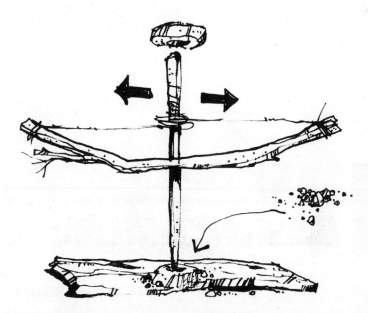

Drawing Enhances Learning

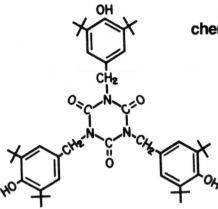

2-Dimensional chemical structure

3-Dimensional chemical structure

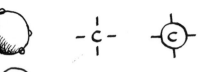

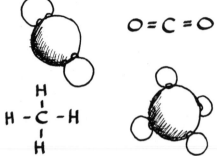

To enable the artist to draw the two- and three- dimensional views of the molecular structure shown, he needed to learn what those relationships were. He needed to know what connected to what and why. He learned about this molecular structure by drawing it.

Likewise, the illustration depicting how to clean a carburetor was done by someone who knew what he was doing. He either knew how to clean it and then did the drawing, or he learned how to clean it by doing the drawing.

3D often shows the relationship between parts better than 2D

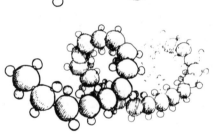

Plastics for Architects and Builders, Albert G. H. Dietz, MIT Press

We draw what we sense, searching for content. To talk as one draws means to reason as one perceives; define as one designs.

Joseph Brunon

164

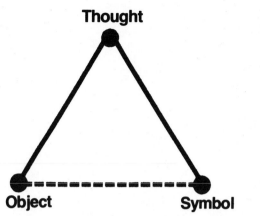

The Meaning of Meaning, Ogden and Richards, Harcourt, Brace and Co.

The triangle depicts communication through abstract terms. We describe a real object in terms which mean that object to our mind but are not the object itself. The word "dog" means a household pet, but the word is not the animal itself—it is instead a verbal term which conveys a meaning to our mind.

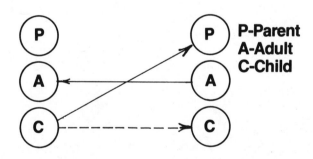

P-Parent
A-Adult
C-Child

The visual expression of transactional relationships makes it easier to understand. The circle and arrows teach concepts that words would have difficulty communicating. The arrows quickly change direction for different relationships.

The drawing about gardening taught the artist how the French method of gardening is done.

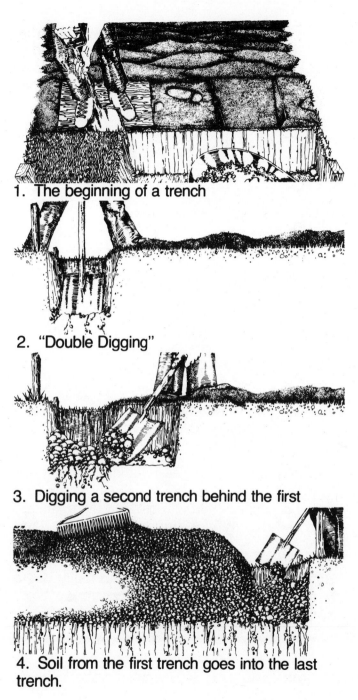

1. The beginning of a trench

2. "Double Digging"

3. Digging a second trench behind the first

4. Soil from the first trench goes into the last trench.

Other Homes and Garbage, illustrated by Bonnie Russel, written by Jim Leckre, Gil Masters, Harry Whitehouse, Lily Young. ©1975 Sierra Club Books

165

**Show only what
is needed to
communicate
the idea**

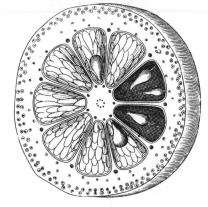

Courtesy of Graphics Magazine

We learn quickly and easily about things by drawing them. The drawing above shows the detail of a seed. You can bet that the botanist who did the drawing understands the anatomy very well.

By drawing the problem you can really begin to see the problem and form possible solutions.

The engineer understands his special pump (bottom right). Visualizing it helped his ability to design and explain its function.

166

Outdoor Plantings

■ OVERHEAD MATERIALS SHOULD BE CHOSEN FOR THEIR PARTICULAR CHARACTERISTICS. AVOID MATERIALS THAT HAVE TENDENCIES TOWARDS DROPPING EXCESSIVE DEBRIS DROOPING OR BREAKING UNDER HEAVY SNOW LOADS, OR WINDS, ETC.

■ MAINTAIN A MINIMUM OF 8'-0" VERTICAL CLEARANCE OVER WALKS, BIKEWAYS, SITTING AREAS, ETC.

■ IMPROPER LOCATION OR POOR MAINTENANCE CAN QUICKLY LEAD TO A REDUCTION OF THE EFFICIENCY OF LIGHTING SYSTEMS.

■ AVOID PLACING HAZARDOUS OR NUISANCE MATERIALS ADJACENT TO WALKWAY OR SITTING AREAS.

■ PLANT MATERIALS MAY AFFECT THE MELTING OF ICE AND SNOW FROM WALKWAYS AND STAIRS. CONSIDER THEIR MATURE SHADOW PATTERNS DURING WINTER MONTHS BEFORE DECIDING ON THEIR FINAL LOCATIONS.

■ MANY TREES WITH SHALLOW OR SURFACE ROOT SYSTEMS WILL HEAVE OR BREAK UP WALKWAY SURFACES. USE CAUTION WHEN CHOOSING THESE VARIETIES AND THEIR SUBSEQUENT LOCATIONS.

■ AVOID PLACING MATERIALS OVER OR NEAR UNDERGROUND UTILITIES. IF THEY HAVE ROOT SYSTEMS THAT CHARACTERISTICALLY CAUSE DAMAGE TO PIPELINES, CABLES, SEWERS, ETC.

■ CREEPING GROUND COVERS, VINES AND OTHER INVASIVE MATERIALS CAN BE TROUBLESOME IF NOT CONTAINED— KEEP THEM OFF BUILDINGS, WALKWAYS STEPS, RAMPS, SIGNS, AND LIGHTING FIXTURES.

Barrier Free Site Design, U.S. Government Publication

By visualizing and making notes the landscape architect was able to more completely understand the components of park design as illustrated here.

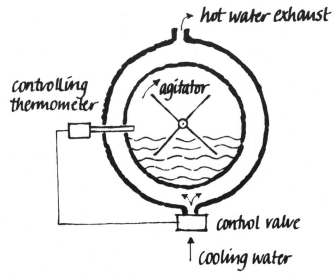

The Design of Design, Gordon L. Clegg, Cambridge University Press

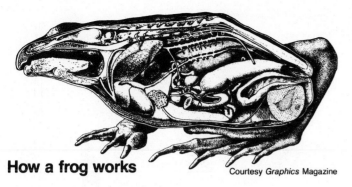

How a frog works

Courtesy *Graphics* Magazine

The anatomy of the frog, the internal combustion engine or the evolution of a valley—these visualizations are tools for learning. They teach not only the viewer, but even more the person who does the drawing.

How an engine works

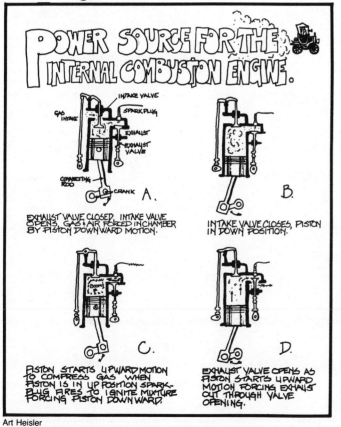

Art Heisler

How landscape evolution works

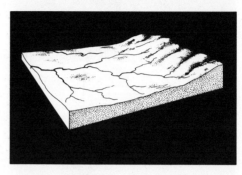

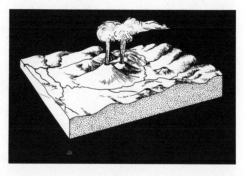

Drawing acts like a filter by removing unnecessary visual elements and only communicating what is needed.

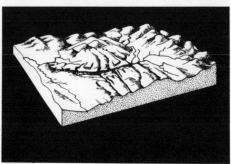

Media Mill, Sat Lake City, Utah

167

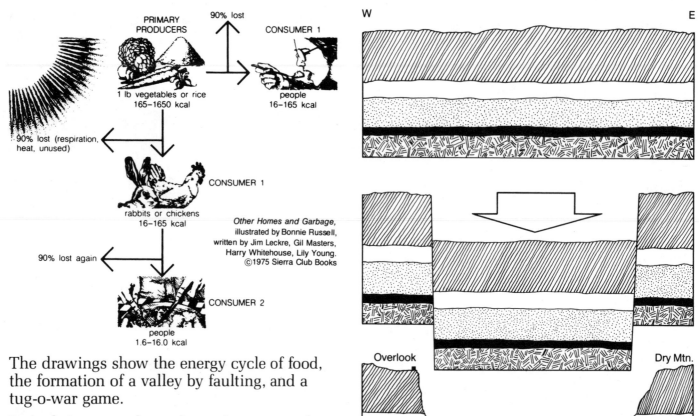

PRIMARY
PRODUCERS

90% lost

CONSUMER 1

1 lb vegetables or rice
165–1650 kcal

people
16–165 kcal

90% lost (respiration, heat, unused)

CONSUMER 1

rabbits or chickens
16–165 kcal

Other Homes and Garbage,
illustrated by Bonnie Russell,
written by Jim Leckre, Gil Masters,
Harry Whitehouse, Lily Young.
©1975 Sierra Club Books

90% lost again

CONSUMER 2

people
1.6–16.0 kcal

W   E

Overlook   Dry Mtn.

Dugway Hollow

Media Mill, Sat Lake City, Utah

The drawings show the energy cycle of food, the formation of a valley by faulting, and a tug-o-war game.

In each instance shown here, the person who did the drawing learned by drawing. He had to become very familiar with what he was portraying in order to communicate it correctly.

Doodle Fun, Alma Heaton, Brigham Young University Press, 1975

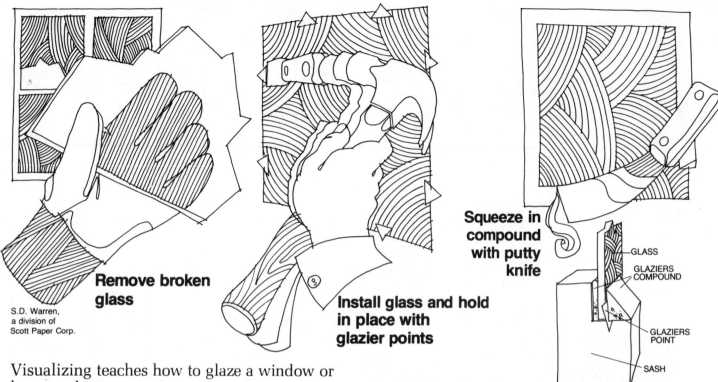

Remove broken glass

Install glass and hold in place with glazier points

Squeeze in compound with putty knife

GLASS

GLAZIERS COMPOUND

GLAZIERS POINT

SASH

Visualizing teaches how to glaze a window or how to plan a game room.

Miss-Hit Pin

Parallel Basketball

Wall Board Table Game Equipment

Wheel Spin Throw

Floor Tennis

Basketball

Tile Shuffle

Hopscotch-In

Doodle Fun, Alma Heaton, Brigham Young University Press, 1975

169

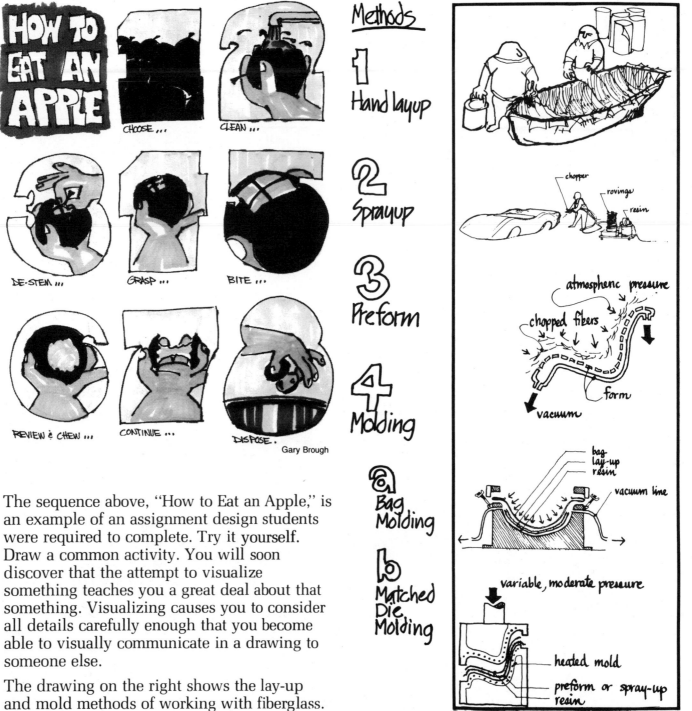

HOW TO EAT AN APPLE

CHOOSE...

CLEAN...

DE-STEM...

GRASP...

BITE...

REVIEW & CHEW...

CONTINUE...

DISPOSE.

Gary Brough

Methods

1 Hand layup

2 Sprayup

3 Preform

4 Molding

ⓐ Bag Molding

ⓑ Matched Die Molding

The sequence above, "How to Eat an Apple," is an example of an assignment design students were required to complete. Try it yourself. Draw a common activity. You will soon discover that the attempt to visualize something teaches you a great deal about that something. Visualizing causes you to consider all details carefully enough that you become able to visually communicate in a drawing to someone else.

The drawing on the right shows the lay-up and mold methods of working with fiberglass.

170

Plastics for Architects and Builders, Albert G. H. Dietz, MIT Press—illustration by Scott Danielson

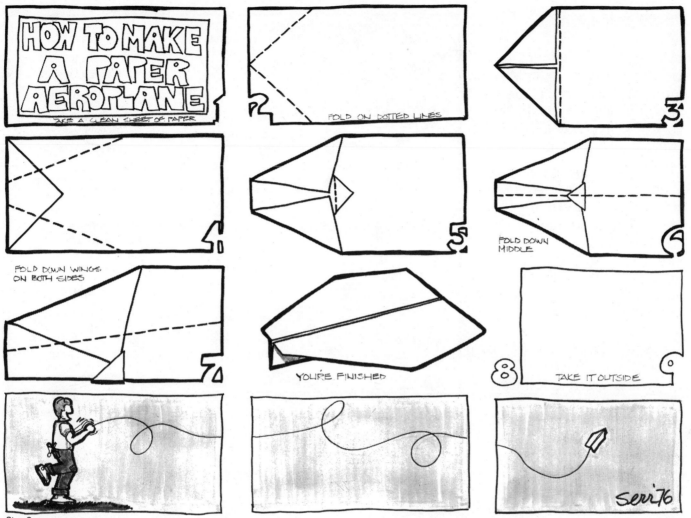

This is another example of a design student
visually depicting a simple activity. You can
be assured that he knew very well how to fold
a paper aeroplane—especially after drawing
the method for you to see.

Visual Note-taking

Taking notes about a given subject can be done in a sort of hieroglyphic form combining drawings and words. It is a very effective way to remember and recall information.

The experiences of a student named Mary demonstrate the effectiveness of visual note-taking. She was getting C's in a psychology class at mid semester in a large university. She wanted to do better but was concerned that she didn't improve no matter how hard she tried. We explained the concept of visual note-taking to her and suggested she give it a try. That was the last we heard of Mary until the semester ended. When grades were released Mary returned to share her experience in visual note-taking with us. She proudly showed an 'A' which she attributed to visual note-taking. She said that visual notes made the entire difference from a 'C' to an 'A', for her.

Another example of the value of visual notes was related by the clergy of a local religious group. He explained that a small child was asked to speak before an adult congregation. To help the child communicate

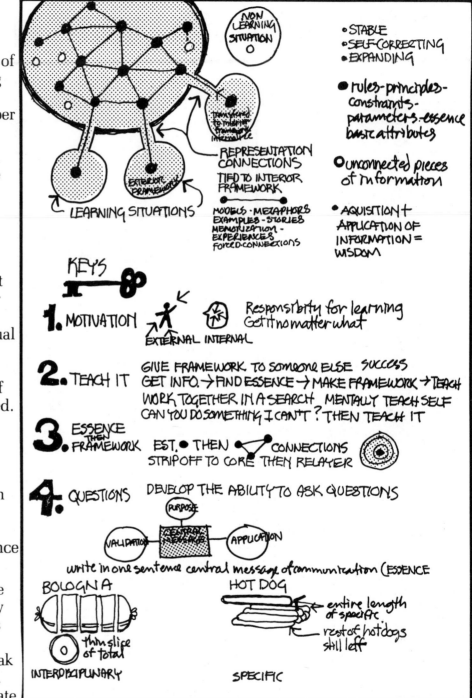

172

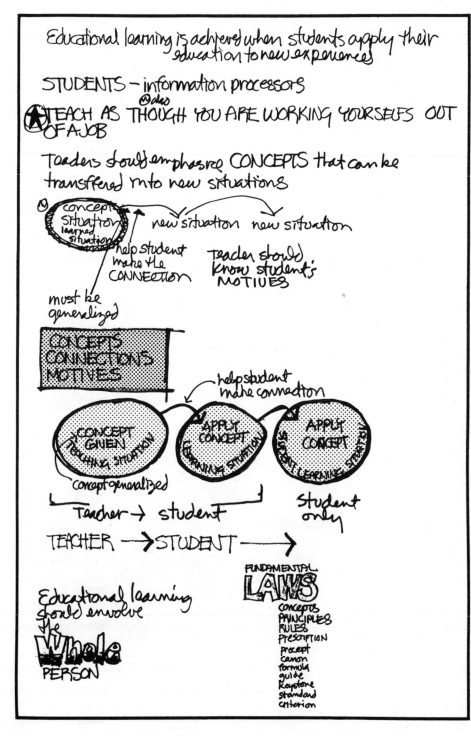

in his own words, his mother prepared visual notes which he could follow. The speech was about doing enough but not becoming overloaded with too many things at one time. The mother drew trucks to illustrate the concept—one truck was empty, one loaded just right and one overloaded so that the back-end slumped down and the front end raised. From these visual notes the child was able to deliver an effective, complete, sincere and natural message. In his own words he expressed what was in his heart . . . and what his notes told him.

Doodling and sketching with your notes will expand your creativity and drawing ability. Visual images are more easily remembered and give more information than words. We use a verbal language but much of our thinking is visual. A written visual language along with our verbal language would make each more effective.

"... there is a basic need for us to 'see' problems in their simplest abstract form in order to better apply our mental abilities."

Paul Laseau

173

174

Architects/Planners Alliance, Salt Lake City, Utah

These drawings are the notes an architect made to help him plan the reconstruction of an older section of Salt Lake City, Utah.

The detailed drawings enabled the architect to plan in advance and avoid costly mistakes.

If you have ever tried to build anything you know the value of detailed visual plans. By drawing detailed plans you can avoid paying for needless errors. Detailed blueprints allow you to correct errors before they happen. They allow you to avoid waste. They enable you to do things right.

175

SPECIAL PROVISIONS FOR THE HANDICAPPED

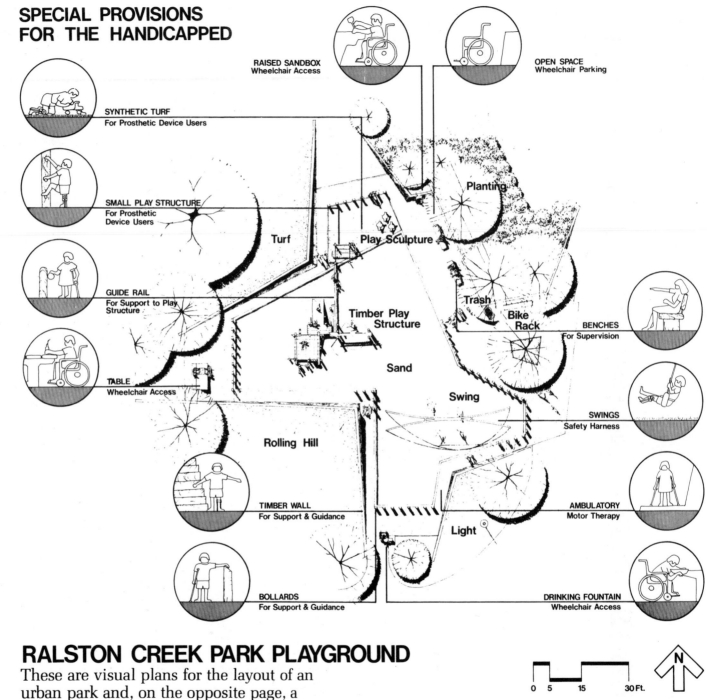

RAISED SANDBOX
Wheelchair Access

OPEN SPACE
Wheelchair Parking

SYNTHETIC TURF
For Prosthetic Device Users

SMALL PLAY STRUCTURE
For Prosthetic
Device Users

GUIDE RAIL
For Support to Play
Structure

TABLE
Wheelchair Access

Planting

Turf

Play Sculpture

Timber Play
Structure

Trash

Bike
Rack

BENCHES
For Supervision

Sand

Swing

SWINGS
Safety Harness

Rolling Hill

TIMBER WALL
For Support & Guidance

AMBULATORY
Motor Therapy

Light

BOLLARDS
For Support & Guidance

DRINKING FOUNTAIN
Wheelchair Access

RALSTON CREEK PARK PLAYGROUND

These are visual plans for the layout of an
urban park and, on the opposite page, a
space station.

0   5   15   30 Ft.

N

176

Herbert Schaal, EDAW Inc., Fort Collins, Colorado

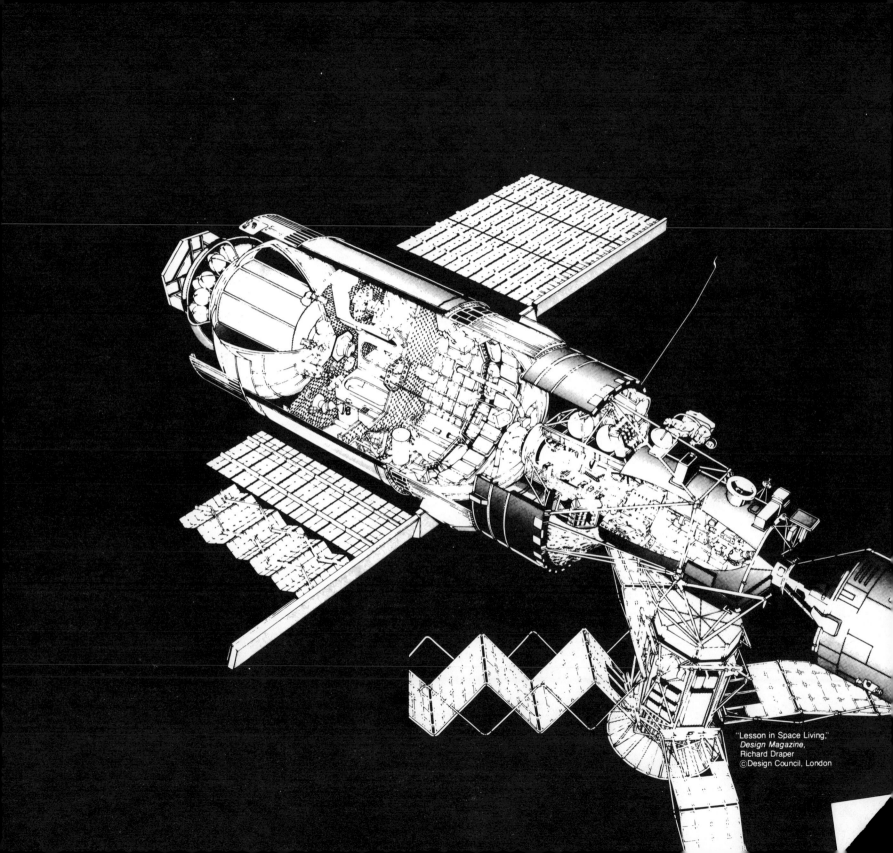

"Lesson in Space Living,"
Design Magazine,
Richard Draper
©Design Council, London

Visual renderings of working objects offer a greater insight than even the real thing. Drawings allow you to see "inside" an object. Without altering or destroying the object, you are able to dissect it and see how it works. You are able to see its structure and how it functions.

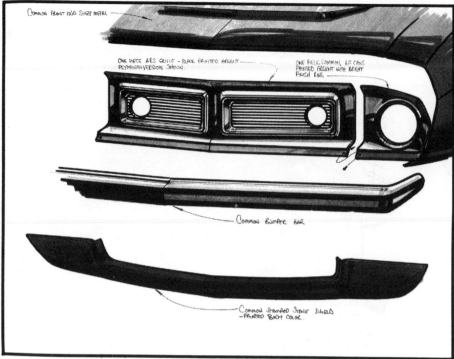

Drawing file, Brigham Young University, Design Department

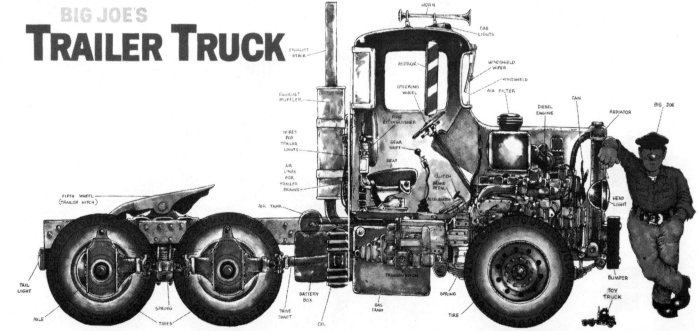

Big Joe's Trailer Truck, Mathiew, Random House, Inc.

178

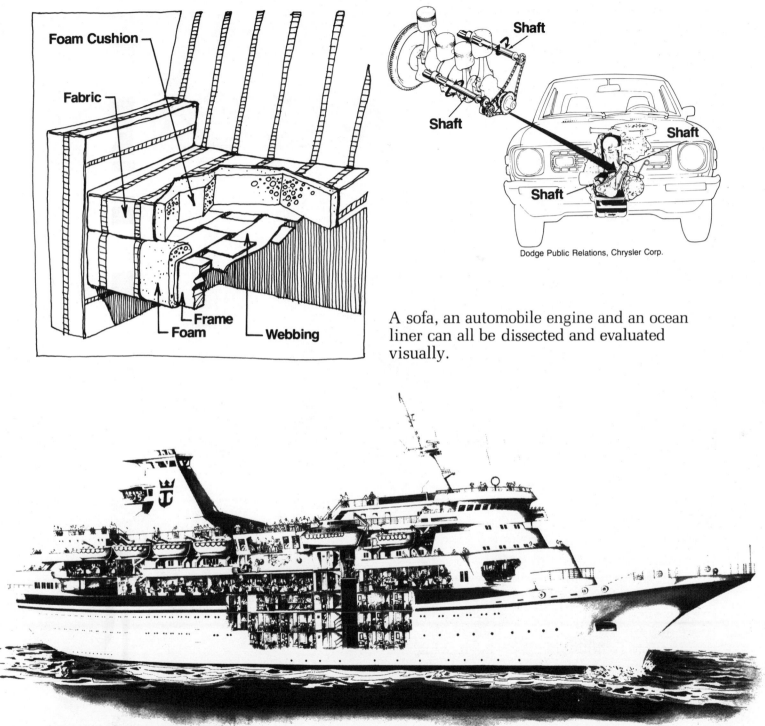

Foam Cushion

Fabric

Frame

Foam

Webbing

Shaft

Shaft

Shaft

Shaft

Dodge Public Relations, Chrysler Corp.

A sofa, an automobile engine and an ocean liner can all be dissected and evaluated visually.

Illustration courtesy of Royal Caribbean Cruise Line

179

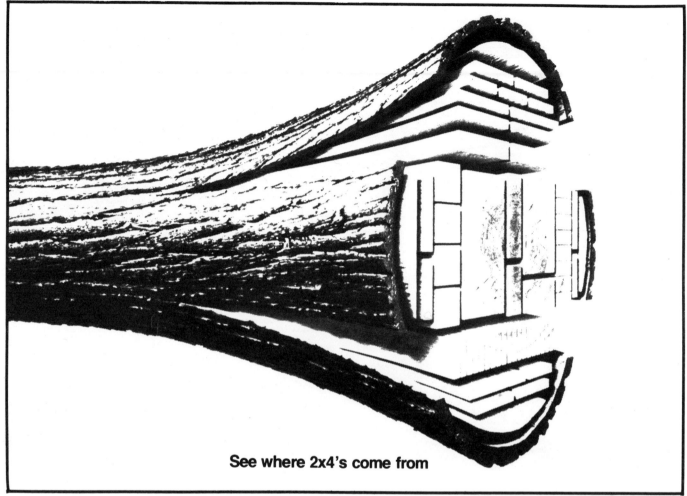

See where 2x4's come from

The drawing of this tree gives an understanding of where our lumber comes from. Without drawing, this kind of understanding would only be possible by first hand observation. Lumber mills do not cut trees as pictured above. Mills cut logs one piece at a time until the log is thoroughly divided into building lumber. The drawing above was not done from a real model but instead was produced from someone's mental visual image.

Drawing often gives us a more thorough and complete view of reality than nature can give us. We not only see nature, but drawing allows us to see what is happening to nature. Drawing sees action and abstraction as well as reality.

180

Our eyes have the ability to see through walls with the help of some drawings. At will, we can see what is happening inside as well as outside a building. We can see the human element living within that immense architectural structure.

Travel Lodge

Draw and see how things fit together

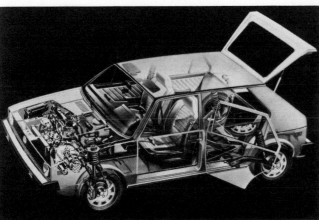

Volkswagen of America, Inc.

Or we can see through the steel shell of an automobile to find trouble spots. Drawings give us X-RAY vision.

181

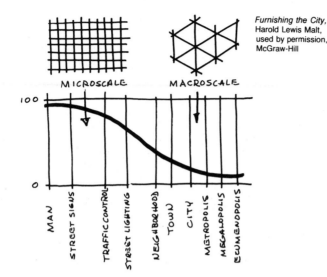

Furnishing the City,
Harold Lewis Malt,
used by permission,
McGraw-Hill

MICROSCALE   MACROSCALE

Visual diagrams and charts are another form of drawing. These flow charts help us see relationships that might otherwise be difficult to understand. They are pictures of thoughts and abstractions rather than objects. Areas of design are expressed here in a microscale—macroscale grid.

The imaginative process of a designer is visualized by this double triangle drawing. Individual ideas enter the top triangle and are evaluated for usable content. The end of the lower triangle represents the elimination of all but the best idea which emerges.

SYNTHESIS
No Judgement
Formulate Ideas
Evaluation: Solutions
Process of Illumination
Best Solution
Sell it to the Boss

Becky Melville

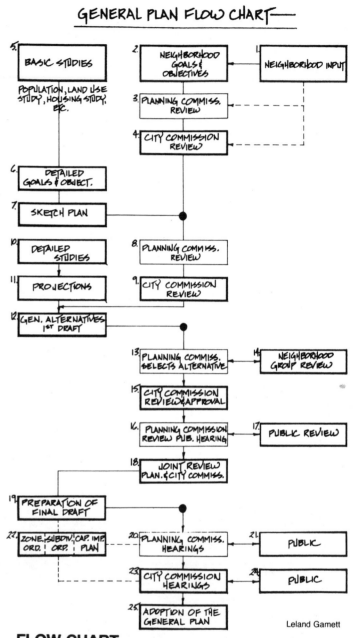

GENERAL PLAN FLOW CHART—

5. BASIC STUDIES
POPULATION, LAND USE STUDY, HOUSING STUDY, ETC.

2. NEIGHBORHOOD GOALS & OBJECTIVES
1. NEIGHBORHOOD INPUT
3. PLANNING COMMISS. REVIEW
4. CITY COMMISSION REVIEW

6. DETAILED GOALS & OBJECT.
7. SKETCH PLAN

10. DETAILED STUDIES
8. PLANNING COMMISS. REVIEW
11. PROJECTIONS
9. CITY COMMISSION REVIEW
12. GEN. ALTERNATIVES 1ST DRAFT

13. PLANNING COMMISS. SELECTS ALTERNATIVE
14. NEIGHBORHOOD GROUP REVIEW
15. CITY COMMISSION REVIEW & APPROVAL
16. PLANNING COMMISSION REVIEW PUB. HEARING
17. PUBLIC REVIEW
18. JOINT REVIEW PLAN. & CITY COMMISS.

19. PREPARATION OF FINAL DRAFT
22. ZONE. SUBDIV. CAP. IMP. ORD. ORD. PLAN
20. PLANNING COMMISS. HEARINGS
21. PUBLIC
23. CITY COMMISSION HEARINGS
24. PUBLIC
25. ADOPTION OF THE GENERAL PLAN

Leland Gamett

FLOW CHART

A city planner uses a visual organizational chart to help explain the operating channels in his city.

182

Ecology Process

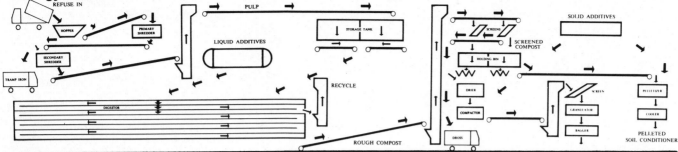

Landgard Process

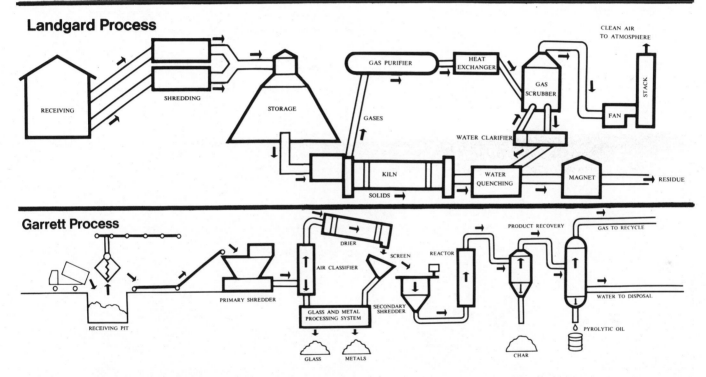

Garrett Process

Reprinted from Summer 1973 Design & Environment

Different methods of processing garbage illustrated through visual rotation.

Different methods of garbage treatment are expressed here. The visual flow charts are a picture and a story all their own.

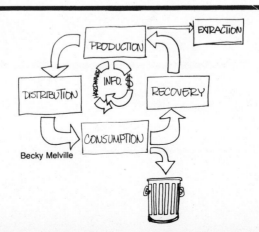

Becky Melville

The lower set of drawings represents the thought process of evaluating a traffic light system. The visual images represent segments of the traffic light evolution for a portion of Salt Lake City. Some of the objects are simply visual images that were triggered in the designer's mind as he was discussing the traffic light evolution.

At top is an abstract visual evaluation of the placement and construction of a house.

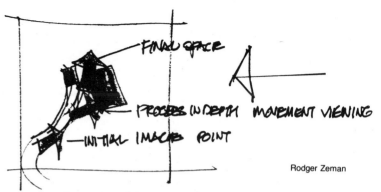

Rodger Zeman

Notes from an idea session

184

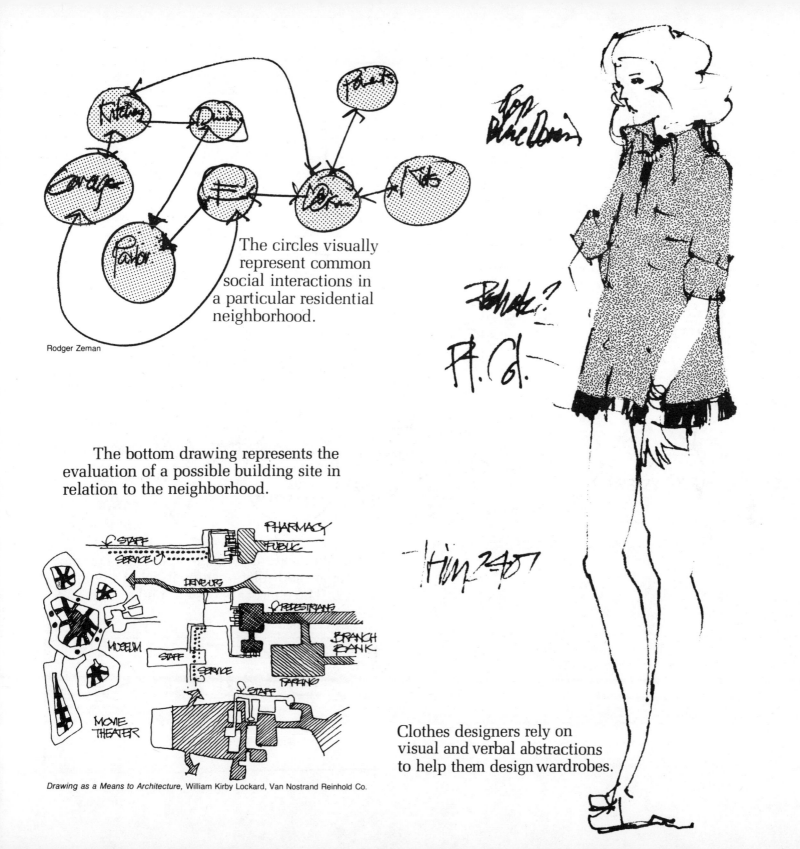

The circles visually represent common social interactions in a particular residential neighborhood.

Rodger Zeman

The bottom drawing represents the evaluation of a possible building site in relation to the neighborhood.

Drawing as a Means to Architecture, William Kirby Lockard, Van Nostrand Reinhold Co.

Clothes designers rely on visual and verbal abstractions to help them design wardrobes.

185

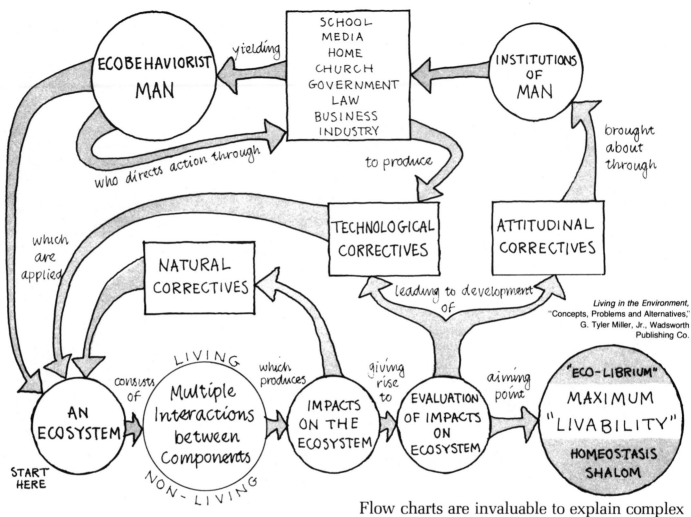

ECOBEHAVIORIST MAN

yielding

SCHOOL
MEDIA
HOME
CHURCH
GOVERNMENT
LAW
BUSINESS
INDUSTRY

INSTITUTIONS OF MAN

who directs action through

to produce

brought about through

TECHNOLOGICAL CORRECTIVES

ATTITUDINAL CORRECTIVES

which are applied

NATURAL CORRECTIVES

leading to development of

Living in the Environment,
"Concepts, Problems and Alternatives,"
G. Tyler Miller, Jr., Wadsworth
Publishing Co.

"ECO-LIBRIUM"
MAXIMUM "LIVABILITY"
HOMEOSTASIS SHALOM

consists of

LIVING
Multiple Interactions between Components
NON-LIVING

which produces

giving rise to

aiming point

AN ECOSYSTEM

START HERE

IMPACTS ON THE ECOSYSTEM

EVALUATION OF IMPACTS ON ECOSYSTEM

Flow charts are invaluable to explain complex processes and relationships in relatively few words. The charts are easy to understand and easy to remember.

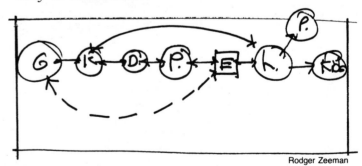

Rodger Zeeman

186

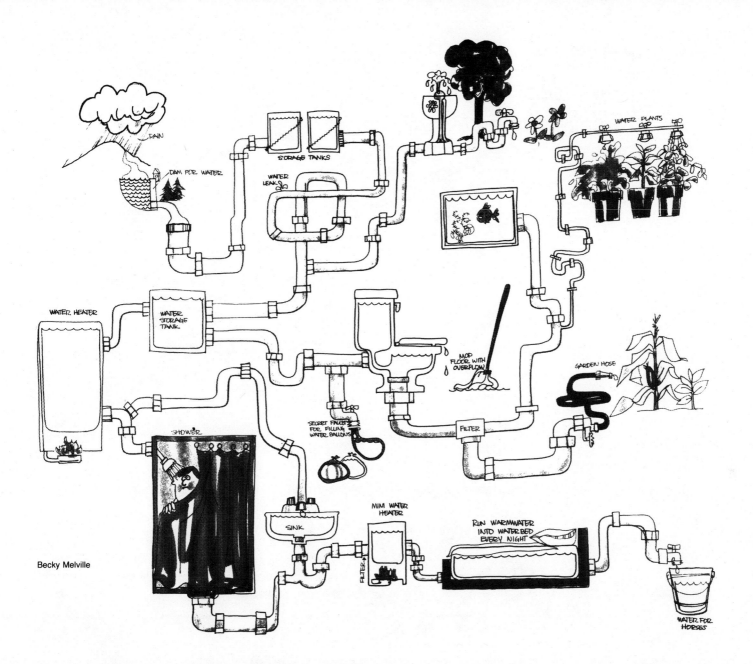

Becky Melville

The plumbing diagram is a flow chart in the "truest" sense of the word. It tells a story of its own.

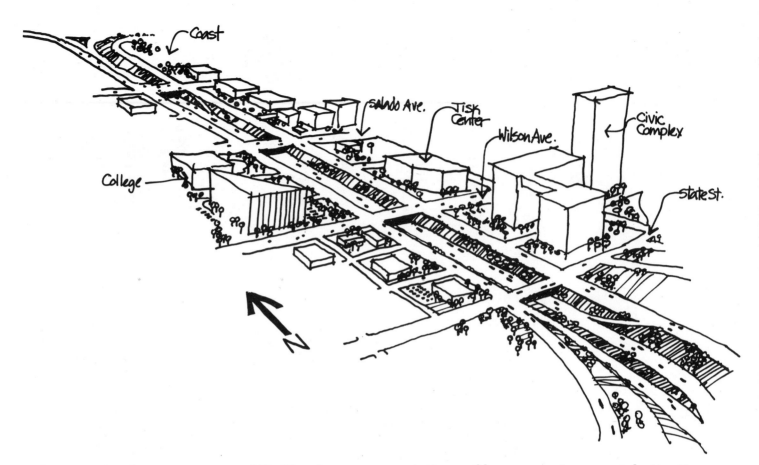

Abstract visual notes are exemplified by these representations of human environmental situations.

Drawing—is it an end, or a means to an end?

The drawings here are taken from Professor McSquared's Calculus Primer. You can bet that the cartoonist understood calculus when he finished illustrating this comic book math book combination. This book, in our opinion, has to be one of the best combinations of both facts and related visual material we've ever seen. It makes learning a difficult subject easier and more effective than the usual dull calculus book.

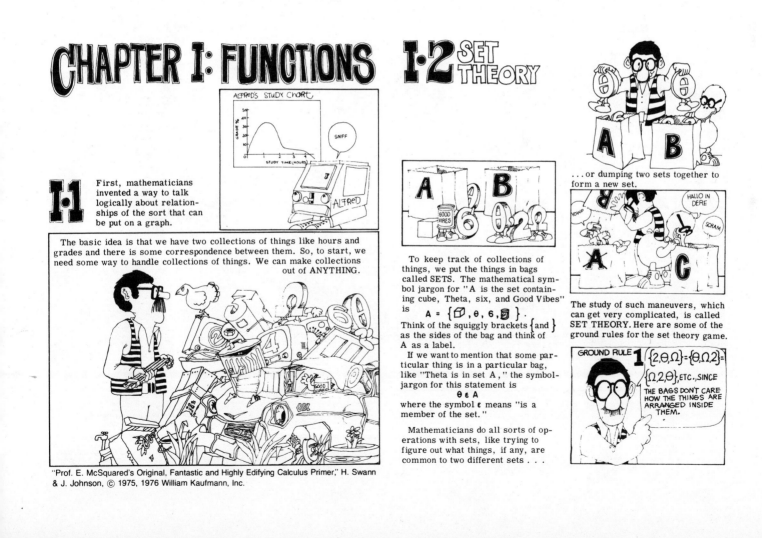

CHAPTER I: FUNCTIONS

I·2 SET THEORY

I·1 First, mathematicians invented a way to talk logically about relationships of the sort that can be put on a graph.

The basic idea is that we have two collections of things like hours and grades and there is some correspondence between them. So, to start, we need some way to handle collections of things. We can make collections out of ANYTHING.

To keep track of collections of things, we put the things in bags called SETS. The mathematical symbol jargon for "A is the set containing cube, Theta, six, and Good Vibes" is

$$A = \{ \square, \theta, 6, \mathbb{J} \}.$$

Think of the squiggly brackets $\{$ and $\}$ as the sides of the bag and think of A as a label.

If we want to mention that some particular thing is in a particular bag, like "Theta is in set A," the symbol-jargon for this statement is

$$\theta \, \varepsilon \, A$$

where the symbol ε means "is a member of the set."

Mathematicians do all sorts of operations with sets, like trying to figure out what things, if any, are common to two different sets . . .

. . . or dumping two sets together to form a new set.

The study of such maneuvers, which can get very complicated, is called SET THEORY. Here are some of the ground rules for the set theory game.

GROUND RULE 1 $\{2,\theta,\Omega\} = \{\theta,\Omega,2\} = \{\Omega,2,\theta\}$, ETC., SINCE THE BAGS DON'T CARE HOW THE THINGS ARE ARRANGED INSIDE THEM.

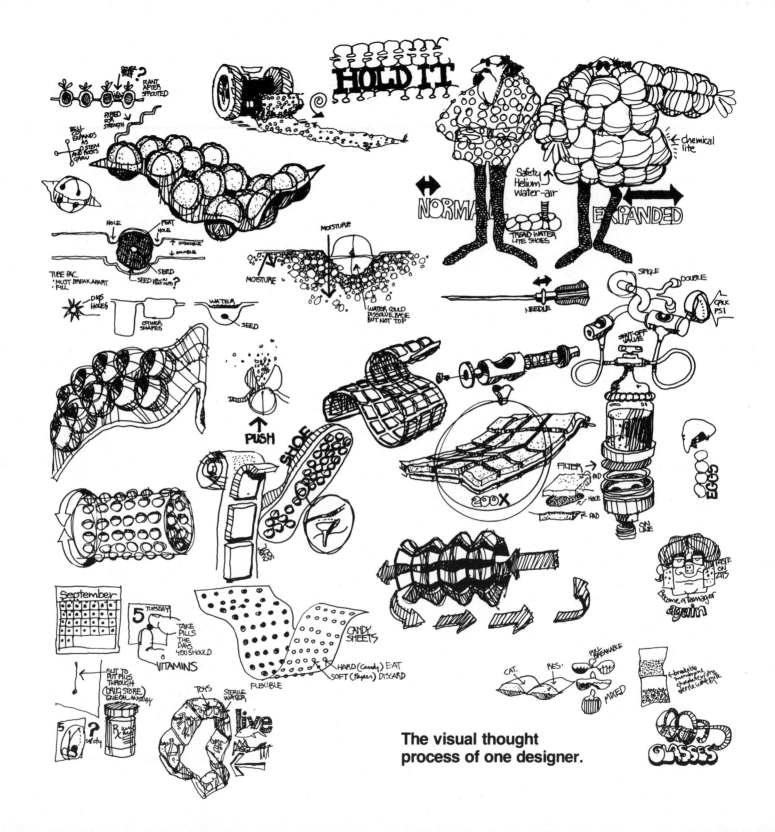

The visual thought
process of one designer.

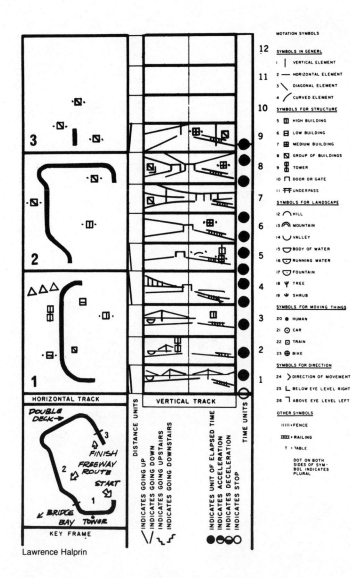

MOTATION SYMBOLS

SYMBOLS IN GENERL
1 | VERTICAL ELEMENT
2 — HORIZONTAL ELEMENT
3 \ DIAGONAL ELEMENT
4 / CURVED ELEMENT

SYMBOLS FOR STRUCTURE
5 HIGH BUILDING
6 LOW BUILDING
7 MEDIUM BUILDING
8 GROUP OF BUILDINGS
9 TOWER
10 DOOR OR GATE
11 UNDERPASS

SYMBOLS FOR LANDSCAPE
12 HILL
13 MOUNTAIN
14 VALLEY
15 BODY OF WATER
16 RUNNING WATER
17 FOUNTAIN
18 TREE
19 SHRUB

SYMBOLS FOR MOVING THINGS
20 HUMAN
21 CAR
22 TRAIN
23 BIKE

SYMBOLS FOR DIRECTION
24 DIRECTION OF MOVEMENT
25 BELOW EYE LEVEL RIGHT
26 ABOVE EYE LEVEL LEFT

OTHER SYMBOLS
= FENCE
= RAILING
T = TABLE

DOT ON BOTH
SIDES OF SYM-
BOL INDICATES
PLURAL

12 11 10 9 8 7 6 5 4 3 2 1

HORIZONTAL TRACK   VERTICAL TRACK

DOUBLE DECK →
3
FINISH
2 FREEWAY ROUTE
START
1
BRIDGE BAY TOWER
KEY FRAME

DISTANCE UNITS
INDICATES GOING UP
INDICATES GOING DOWN
INDICATES GOING UPSTAIRS
INDICATES GOING DOWNSTAIRS

TIME UNITS
INDICATES UNIT OF ELAPSED TIME
INDICATES ACCELERATION
INDICATES DECELERATION
INDICATES STOP

Lawrence Halprin

Motation—a graphic language of movement through space.

The visual representations here are a method of evaluating a driving experience. A landscape architect has produced a visual language to help him remember and see in his mind a previous driving experience. It is like a language of hieroglyphics.

1. The can ascends a curved ramp.

5. Nearing the civic center

8. Car enters a rather cubistic processional

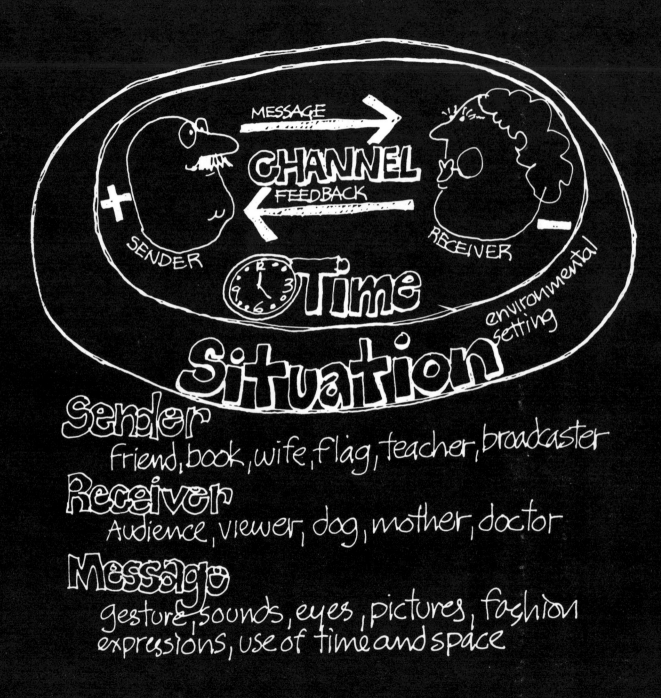

Sender
friend, book, wife, flag, teacher, broadcaster

Receiver
Audience, viewer, dog, mother, doctor

Message
gesture, sounds, eyes, pictures, fashion
expressions, use of time and space

Communication

75% of each waking day is spent in some form of communication.

Drawing can be a valuable tool for communicating. This portion of the book deals with various aspects of drawing as a means of communicating.

The previous section—notation—discussed the concept of a person talking to himself visually through drawing. The notation section conveyed the concept that the act of drawing is a tool for understanding and learning for the person doing the drawing.

This section—communication—concerns itself with the idea that drawing is a valuable tool for communicating. Drawing is a means of conveying a message from one person to another.

Communication usually involves a sender, a receiver, a message and often feedback.

The sender in a communicating situation can be many things. It can be a person, an animal or an inanimate object like a radio, a television or a movie. It is the means by which a message is transmitted.

The receiver of communicated material is the person who accepts a message from the sender.

The message communicated is the meaning of sounds, pictures, words, drawings, gestures and expressions received from the sender.

Drawing is unique in the scheme of communicating in that the sender and the message can be one and the same. A drawing itself is often the sender. The fact that you look at a drawing is sufficient to send the message, and the drawing is the message that you see.

193

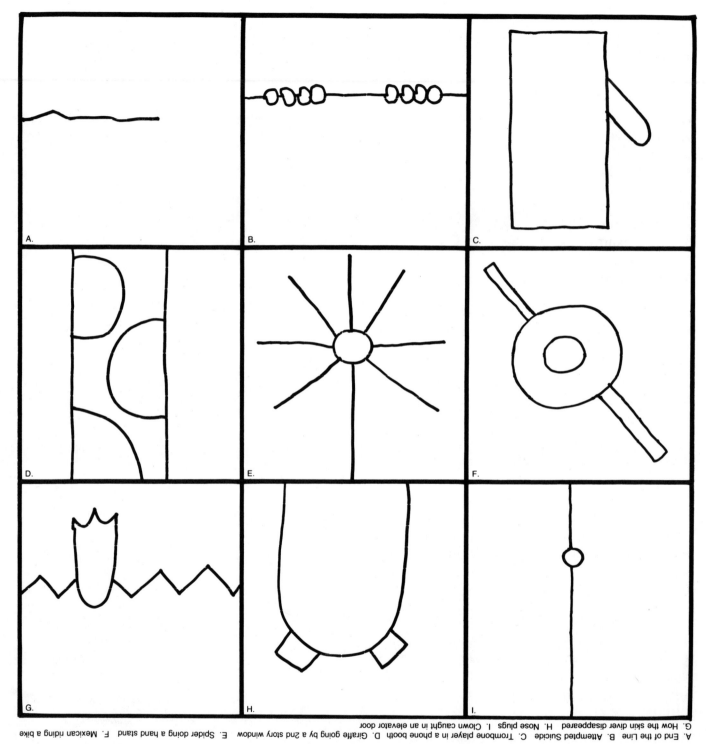

A. End of the Line B. Attempted Suicide C. Trombone player in a phone booth D. Giraffe going by a 2nd story window E. Spider doing a hand stand F. Mexican riding a bike
G. How the skin diver disappeared H. Nose plugs I. Clown caught in an elevator door

Let's consider how our perception of things affects communication. Just for fun, can you identify the objects shown on the previous page: (Answers are listed on the bottom of the opposite pages.)

We all perceive things differently. We often see what we expect to see or what we want to see rather than the real image or message. For example, a bullfighter sees a bull through different eyes and for different reasons than does a beef cattle rancher, an animal hide tanner, a butcher, or a cow or another bull. Another example is demonstrated by the reaction French school children had to certain English words. They liked "Diarrhea" as a pretty woman's name and chose "Cellar Door" as the most beautiful sounding word. You speak English—do you perceive them the same way?

We often interpret information according to the context in which we receive it. Look at the circles. You will notice one circle surrounded by four smaller circles and another circle surrounded by four larger circles. These two center circles probably look different in size to you. But if you will measure closely you'll find they are identical. It is their surroundings, the context in which we find them, that influences our different perception of them.

90% of all communication goes through the eyes.

The cartoon shows a man explaining his new invention. The mother sees her son on a pedestal. One man sees himself in a limousine spending the money that will come from the invention. Another man could care less. And all of them are receiving a different message. What is important here is the discrepancy between what the drawing the man is holding is suppose to communicate and what it actually did communicate.

195

Communicating is the transfer of ideas. Usually we imply that communicating is done between people. Drawing allows us to communicate ideas to ourselves (see the notation section) as well as to others. Drawing enables us to share ideas with one other person or a group of people.

Ideation and notation is visually talking to oneself. Communication is visually talking to others.

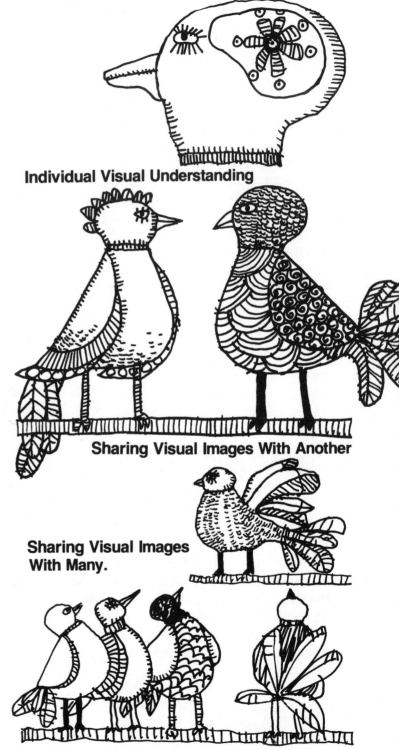

Individual Visual Understanding

Sharing Visual Images With Another

Sharing Visual Images With Many.

All drawing is an abstraction. A picture of a bird is not a bird though you may receive much the same information and feelings from the drawing as from the actual bird. A graph of personal relationships may communicate a great deal of psychology, but it is not the people or their personal feelings. Drawing is only a language in dealing with what is perceived as real, not reality itself.

The essence of drawing lies in the awareness of it only as an instrument and then using that instrument to communicate to oneself and to others.

Sketching and drawing can use concrete or abstract imagery, varying the degree of visual abstraction to the particular situation in which it is used.

The man on the ladder is a graphic illustration (in its own abstract way) of what we are talking about. The ladder represents a scale of

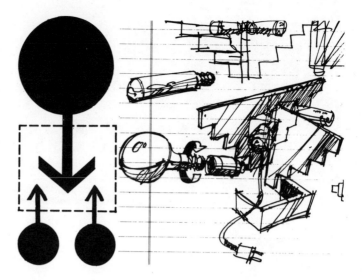

abstraction—one can go up or down depending on the need—up to very abstract visual concepts or down to more concrete images. For the amount of abstraction and reality you use in your drawings, decide where you would be located on the ladder of visual abstraction and then apply this knowledge to your particular drawing situation. Use drawing to communicate, but understand its limits and possibilities. In many circumstances drawing has proven itself one of the most effective language tools man has ever used.

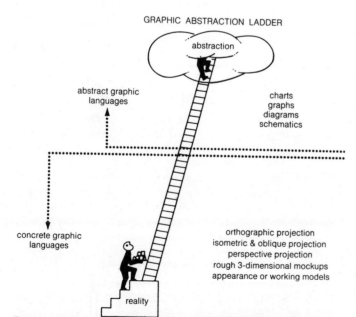

GRAPHIC ABSTRACTION LADDER

abstraction

abstract graphic languages

charts
graphs
diagrams
schematics

concrete graphic languages

orthographic projection
isometric & oblique projection
perspective projection
rough 3-dimensional mockups
appearance or working models

reality

Experiences in Visual Thinking, Robert McKim, Brooks/Cole Publishing Co.

Artists put their talents to good use when they act on the assumption that every art work is a statement about something.
R. Arnheim

IMAGE
Transfer & Storage

The end result of visual communication is to transfer your ideas into someone else's mind. The image used is secondary to the desired result. The image is important only as it relates to what you are trying to say.

If you want to communicate, first become aware of who you are talking to. Is it a child, a professor, a plumber or a taxicab driver? Each viewer is different and so are his perspectives of the circumstances that surround his life.

Next consider the context in which you will present your drawings. Is it at the museum, before a small group or on television?

Decide what you want to accomplish. What are the images you want to develop in the viewer's mind's eye? The most important pictures you paint are in the viewer's mind, not on your paper. People create much better pictures in their own minds than you can ever sketch or draw on paper.

And finally comes the drawing itself. The drawing depends on the viewer, the viewing situation and what you want to communicate to be successful. Each of these things dictates how the drawing will be done and the way it will look.

I know you believe you understand what you think I said, but I am not sure you realize that what you hear is not what I meant.

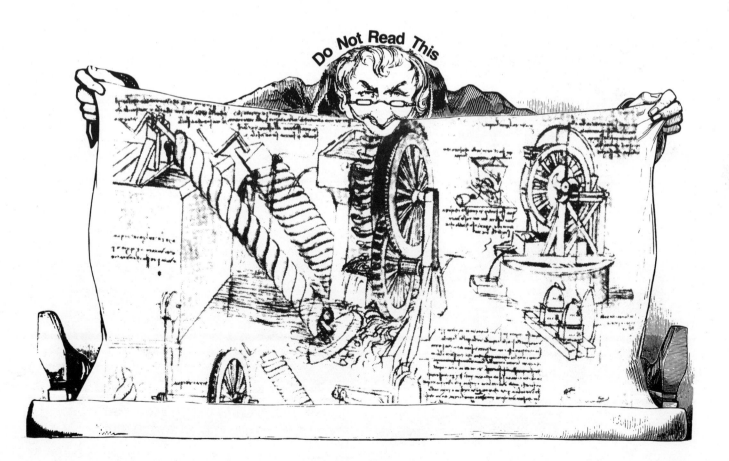

History is a subject for which drawing can provide a primary form of visual understanding. Many aspects of history have no photographic records and only skimpy written records—or even none at all. But by piecing bits of information together an historican can draw a picture of what things were like. He can see how the Anasazi Indians lived when the only records available are the partial structure of an old dwelling and some other artifacts. How pioneers lived in a settlement that vanished long ago can be convincingly re-created in appropriate drawings.

the anasazi

Five hundred years before Escalante and his party explored this country, another people lived here. Known as the Anasazi ("Ancient Ones" in Navajo), they occupied these canyons and mesas from 46 B.C. to 1300 A.D. They built stone houses, farmed plots of corn, beans and squash, and made fine pottery and baskets. In the later part of the Thirteenth Century these ancient Pueblo Indians abandoned the area leaving numerous villages, such as the one depicted here, deserted and subject to the elements.

The Media Mill, Salt Lake City, Utah

200

The Media Mill, Salt Lake City, Utah

This illustration communicates a narrow gauge railroad track and the engine that traveled on that track in the development of the west.

Gerreld Pulsipher

Painstaking scientific research, drawings and artistic reconstructions enable us to know what many dinosaurs were like. Scientists and artists have been able to visualize them and us from data and clues obtained from petrified bone fragments and other fossil records, including habitats.

201

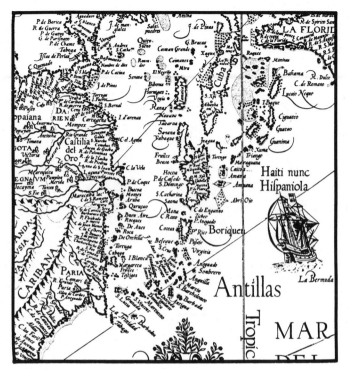

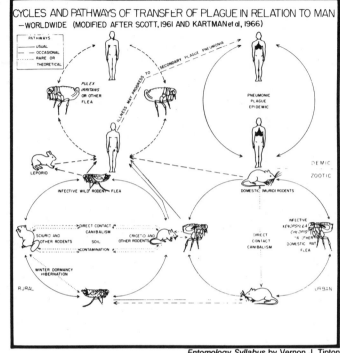

Entomology Syllabus by Vernon J. Tipton

The content of an ancient map is history itself. The map communicates centuries-old thinking and geographical understanding.

Or we can learn about more "modern" things such as health information. The top illustration depicts the spread of bubonic plague. The bottom series of illustrations demonstrates exercises for the over-60 age group.

The Fitness Challenge, U.S. Government Publication

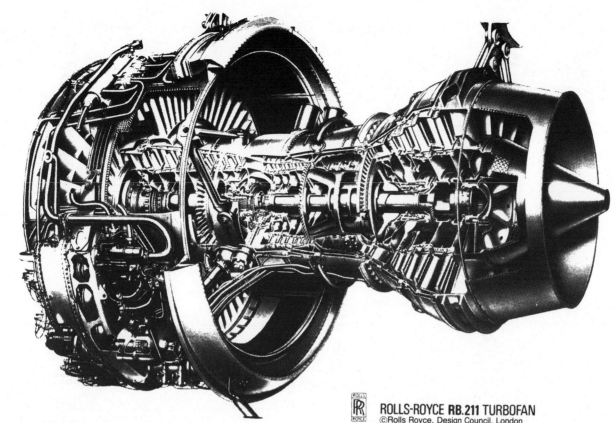

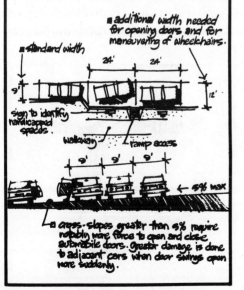

Turbofan engine labels:

ROLLS-ROYCE **RB.211** TURBOFAN
©Rolls Royce, Design Council, London

Parking diagram labels:

■ additional width needed for opening doors and for maneuvering of wheelchairs.

■ standard width

24'   24'

9'   12'

sign to identify handicapped spaces.

walkway   ramp access

9'   9'   9'

← 5% max

■ cross-slopes greater than 5% require notably more force to open and close automobile doors. greater damage is done to adjacent cars when door swings open more suddenly.

Barrier Free Site Design, U.S. Government Publication

Drawing can communicate how things work. Above is the analysis of a turbofan engine. Below is a visual explanation of an automobile parking situation.

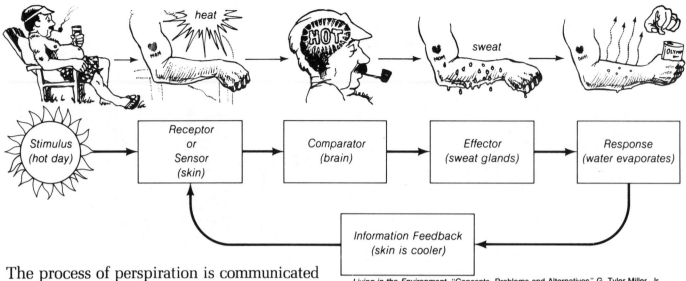

heat

sweat

| Stimulus (hot day) | → | Receptor or Sensor (skin) | → | Comparator (brain) | → | Effector (sweat glands) | → | Response (water evaporates) |

Information Feedback (skin is cooler)

The process of perspiration is communicated simply and easily through visual explanation.

Living in the Environment, "Concepts, Problems and Alternatives," G. Tyler Miller, Jr., Wadsworth Publishing Co.

Strip mining is visually communicated here. Bulldozers and power shovels clear away trees, brush, and topsoil (overburden). Explosive charges loosen the coal deposits, and power shovels or auger drills load the coal into trucks in the pit. Strip mining exposes cross sections of the earth's crust (the highwalls), and the discarded overburden is piled into long rows called spoil banks.

A visual enlargement of the venom-delivering mechanism of a centipede helps us understand how it works.

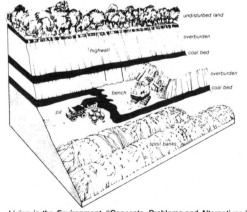

undisturbed land
overburden
highwall
coal bed
overburden
coal bed
bench
pit
spoil banks

Living in the Environment, "Concepts, Problems and Alternatives," G. Tyler, Jr., Wadsworth Publishing Co.

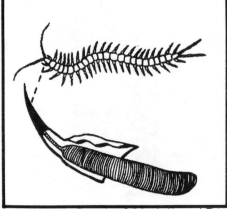

Entomology Syllabus by Vernon J. Tipton

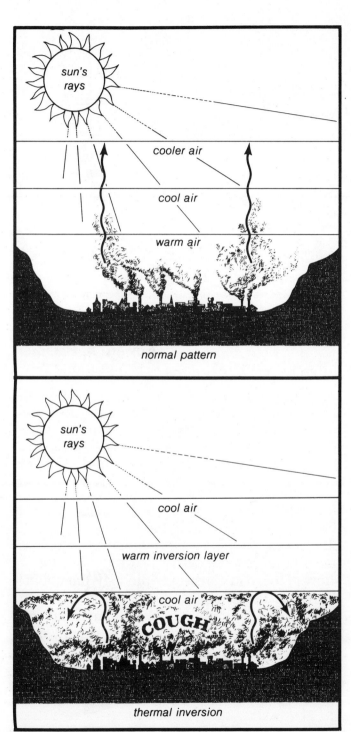

sun's rays

cooler air

cool air

warm air

normal pattern

sun's rays

cool air

warm inversion layer

cool air

COUGH

thermal inversion

Living in the Environment, "Concepts, Problems and Alternatives," G. Tyler, Jr., Wadworth Publishing Co.

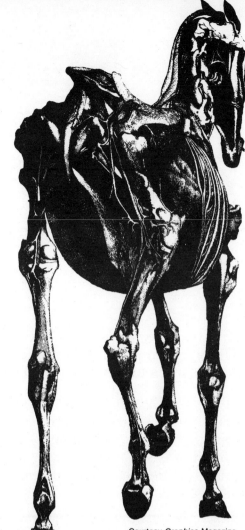

Courtesy *Graphics* Magazine

The dissected horse communicates to our mind a very unique view of anatomy. We can understand the anatomy as it relates to motion by the use of drawing. The horse is shown here moving as though it were walking even when it is not. A truly dissected horse would be a lifeless carcass on a dissecting table.

The simplified drawing of a thermal inversion helps us understand about smog. The drawing visually communicates a concept that would require many words to communicate verbally.

205

Learning Through Play, Jean Marzollo and Janice Lloyd, Harper & Row, Publishers, Inc.

Graphic components in sequence nearly always surpass the single symbol or picture in conveying information or vital experience.

Edward A. Hamilton

If you're alive, your experiences are constantly changing. You do not perceive life as a single picture, but as a continually changing scene. Drawing is static and usually only a single frame while life is more like a motion picture of forever changing frames.

For drawings to be most successful they often must be communicated as a sequence showing the linear order of an idea. This way the viewer can see the progressive development and explanation of concepts that a single picture can't possibly communicate.

How would Peanuts be as a cartoon if it had only one frame? It is a cartoon that needs the entire sequence of each strip and even previous strips in order to work.

The drawings at the top of this page and on the next page are sequential in nature. The explanation of how to fix the broken leg of a chair (far right side of page 207) needs all the different sequential parts to be effective.

Without each segment (the clothespin; how the wood chip is inserted into the brace; how the brace is inserted into the leg; how the legs are drawn together) the communicated message would be incomplete.

People often look at art as something you hang on a wall. They see it as a show piece or house decoration. This stereotyping of drawings often leads people to assume that drawing has one single purpose—that the drawing is for show. This also causes people to assume that drawings are always single pieces of art when in reality some drawings need many different parts or sequential illustrations to convey a single message. A child's story-book which relies heavily on illustration to convey the story is an example of sequential drawings.

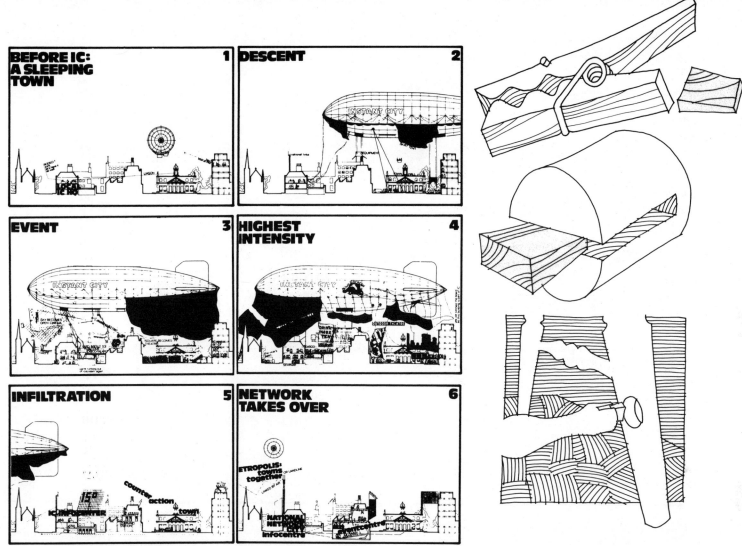

Archigram, Peter Cook, Studio Vista Publishers

The illustrations involving the blimp need
more than one drawing to tell the whole story.
It takes all six illustrations.

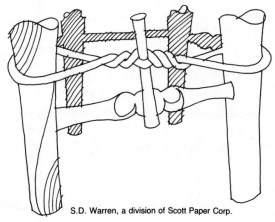

S.D. Warren, a division of Scott Paper Corp.

207

Mark Stehrenberger, Illustrator/Designer, La Crescenta, California

The sequence of all the vans above is
necessary to communicate the evolution of the
vehicle.

The space shuttle is concisely and accurately
communicated through a sequence of
drawings in the composite picture on the
following page.

The drawings
are views of
what you would
see if you
traveled through
the complex
(left) and stopped
to look at each
place where an
arrow is shown.

"Townscape," Gordon Cullen, Copyright 1961 by Architectual Press, London, reprinted by
permission of Van Nostrand Reinhold Co.

208

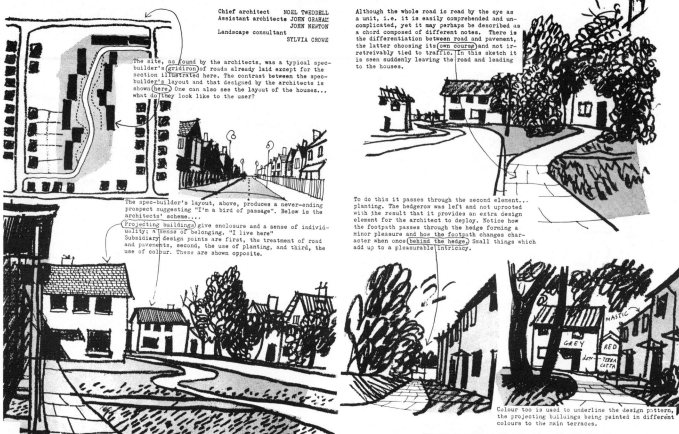

REDGRAVE RD. BASILDON NEW TOWN

Chief architect   NOEL TWEDDELL
Assistant architects JOHN GRAHAM
                    JOHN NEWTON
Landscape consultant
                   SYLVIA CROWE

The site, as found by the architects, was a typical spec-builder's gridiron of roads already laid except for the section illustrated here. The contrast between the spec-builder's layout and that designed by the architects is shown here. One can also see the layout of the houses... what do they look like to the user?

The spec-builder's layout, above, produces a never-ending prospect suggesting "I'm a bird of passage". Below is the architects' scheme....
Projecting buildings give enclosure and a sense of individuality; a sense of belonging. "I live here"
Subsidiary design points are first, the treatment of road and pavements, second, the use of planting, and third, the use of colour. These are shown opposite.

Although the whole road is read by the eye as a unit, i.e. it is easily comprehended and uncomplicated, yet it may perhaps be described as a chord composed of different notes. There is the differentiation between road and pavement, the latter choosing its own course and not irretrievably tied to traffic. In this sketch it is seen suddenly leaving the road and leading to the houses.

To do this it passes through the second element... planting. The hedgerow was left and not uprooted with the result that it provides an extra design element for the architect to deploy. Notice how the footpath passes through the hedge forming a minor pleasure and how the footpath changes character when once behind the hedge. Small things which add up to a pleasurable intricacy.

Colour too is used to underline the design pattern, the projecting buildings being painted in different colours to the main terraces.

MORAL Townscape is seen here not as decoration, not as a style or a device for filling up empty spaces with cobbles: it is seen as the art of using raw materials—houses, trees and roads—to create a lively and human scene.

Townscape, © 1961 by Architectural Press, London, reprinted by permission of Van Nostrand Reinhold Co.

Words and sequential renderings tell the story of a planned architectural living center. In simple language, the communique above demonstrates the "feel" of a proposed development. The sequence helps the viewer put himself into the proposal as a participant in planning.

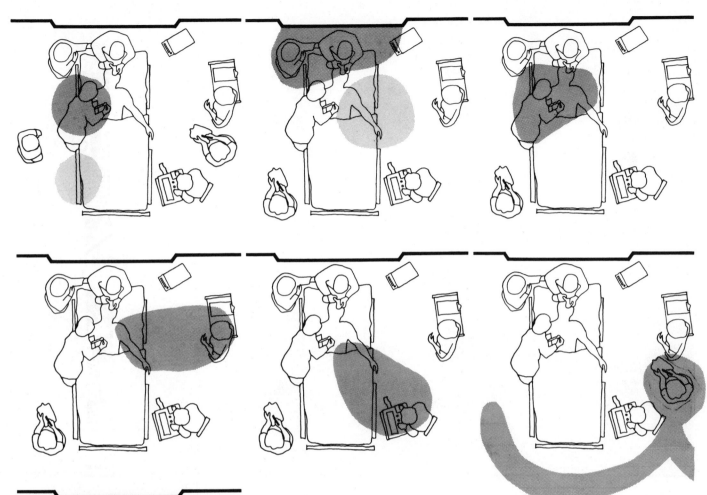

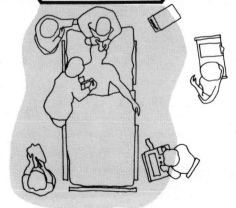

The drawings illustrate a concept in cardiac care. The diagrams speak both to architects and medical personnel. The situation above visually analyzes each member of an operating medical team. Shaded areas indicate principal work spaces needed for each attending medical person.

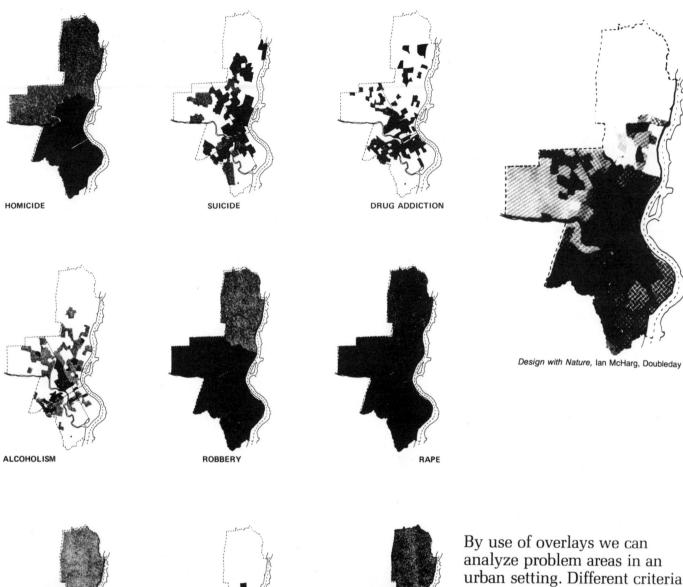

HOMICIDE

SUICIDE

DRUG ADDICTION

ALCOHOLISM

ROBBERY

RAPE

Design with Nature, Ian McHarg, Doubleday

AGGRAVATED ASSAULT

JUVENILE DELINQUENCY

INFANT MORTALITY

By use of overlays we can analyze problem areas in an urban setting. Different criteria are studied and plotted according to severity. As the overlays pile on top of each other, certain locations appear obviously darker or lighter. This visual analysis of an urban setting quickly isolates areas of prime concern.

212

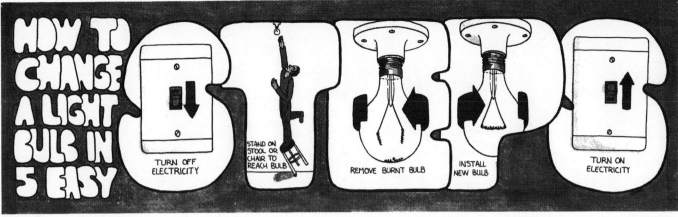

HOW TO CHANGE A LIGHT BULB IN 5 EASY STEPS

TURN OFF ELECTRICITY

STAND ON STOOL OR CHAIR TO REACH BULB

REMOVE BURNT BULB

INSTALL NEW BULB

TURN ON ELECTRICITY

Gary Israel

These self-explanatory visual sequences were done by design students.

how to make orange juice

1 gather materials

2 cut

3 twist

4 pour

Donna Martin

213

UNDERGROUND ARCHITECTURE

Presentation of Ideas

These illustrations provide a stylized visual glance at proposed underground architecture. Sequence makes the drawings more explicit and meaningful.

Visual presentation of material, proposals and concepts is a good way to communicate information to others. Visual presentations can be appealing, informative and easily understood.

The next several pages contain portions of visual presentations. A picture truly can be worth a thousand words.

The reverse (black and white line) illustrations above are loose and abstract, yet they clearly

214

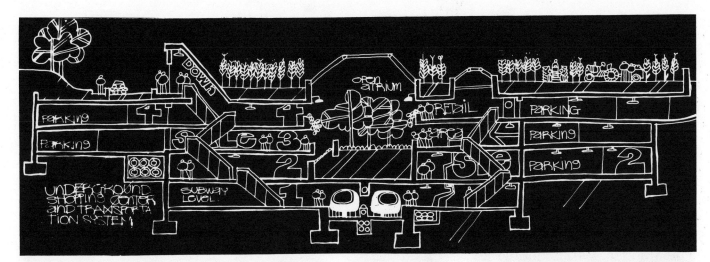

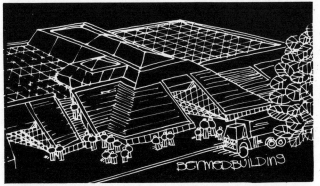

Jim Lewis

convey the message of a massive underground
structure. The small
illustrations below are
also of underground
buildings.

Malcolm Wells

215

The architectural renderings add a second depth to our understanding by showing two views at one time. The top illustration enables us to see the room as we normally would see it. The plan below helps us see the whole picture. We are able to look at the floor plan as people see it and as birds would see it from above. Both illustrations help each other. Since the room is so large, it needs an overall view to give the whole picture. And at the same time the plan as seen from above needs the clarification of an eye level view to give the room a real living feeling.

BEFORE - applying the street graphic system

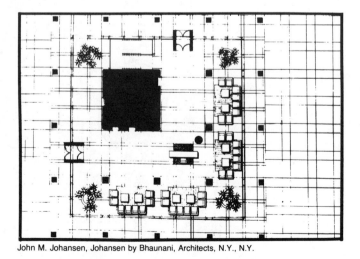

John M. Johansen, Johansen by Bhaunani, Architects, N.Y., N.Y.

AFTER
Drawing by Roger Bradfield, *Street Graphics* William R. Ewald & Daniel R. Mandelker. The American Society of Landscape Architects Foundation.

Before and after pictures give a natural sequence for visual evaluation. They provide a basis for comparison.

216

Levolor Inc.

This rendering of a room setting helps give
visual meaning as explained on the previous
page. Notice the overlapping of items, the use
of shadows to strengthen composition and the
use of detail in the blinds to emphasize them.
This room setting provides a good way to
present venetian blinds in a positive way.

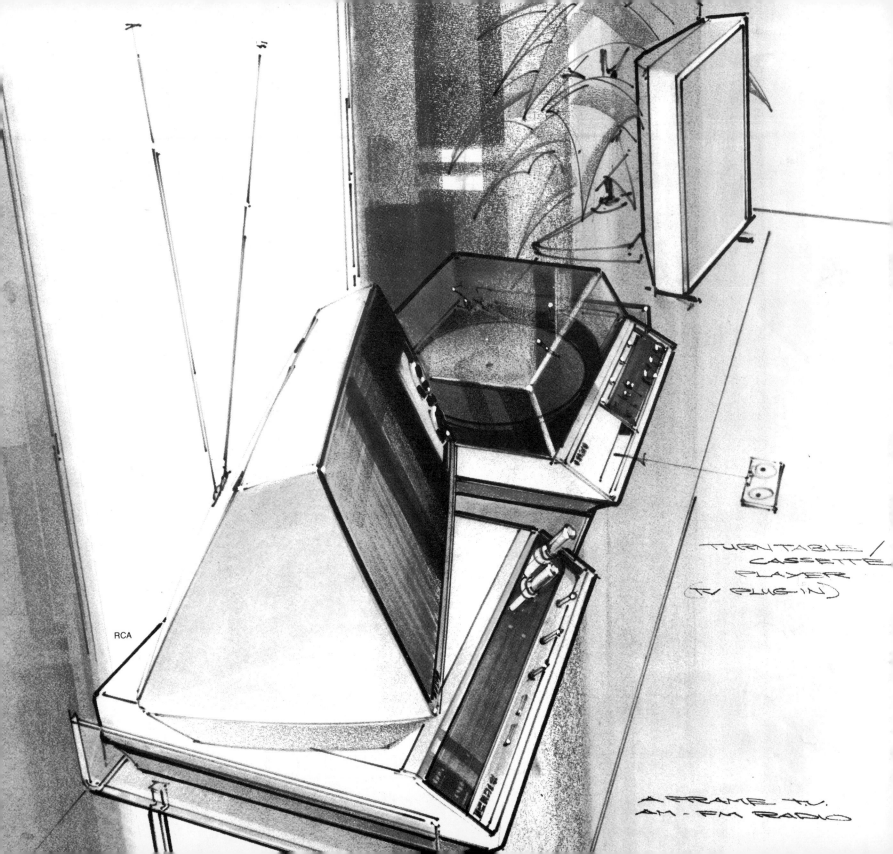

RCA

TURNTABLE /
CASSETTE
PLAYER
(TV PLUG-IN)

A-FRAME TV.
AM-FM RADIO

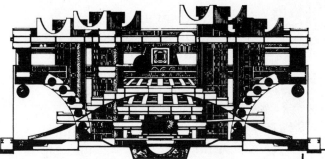

Arcology: The City in the Image of Man, Paolo Soleri, MIT Press

The drawing above is a concept of future building techniques to help create more efficient and humane cities. It is a city within a city.

A superbly detailed illustration of a thistle helps botanists identify it in its natural setting.

As the title indicates, the sequence of drawings and descriptive words below shows how to make paper.

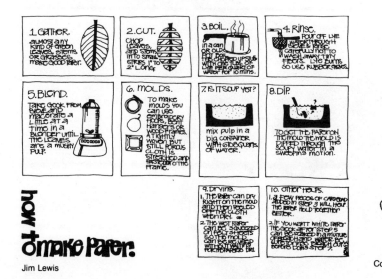

Jim Lewis

Courtesy of Graphics Magazine

The drawings here are excellent examples of visual communication. Many styles are employed to give feeling and tell the desired story.

This shows a modular building system designed to integrate well with an alpine setting.

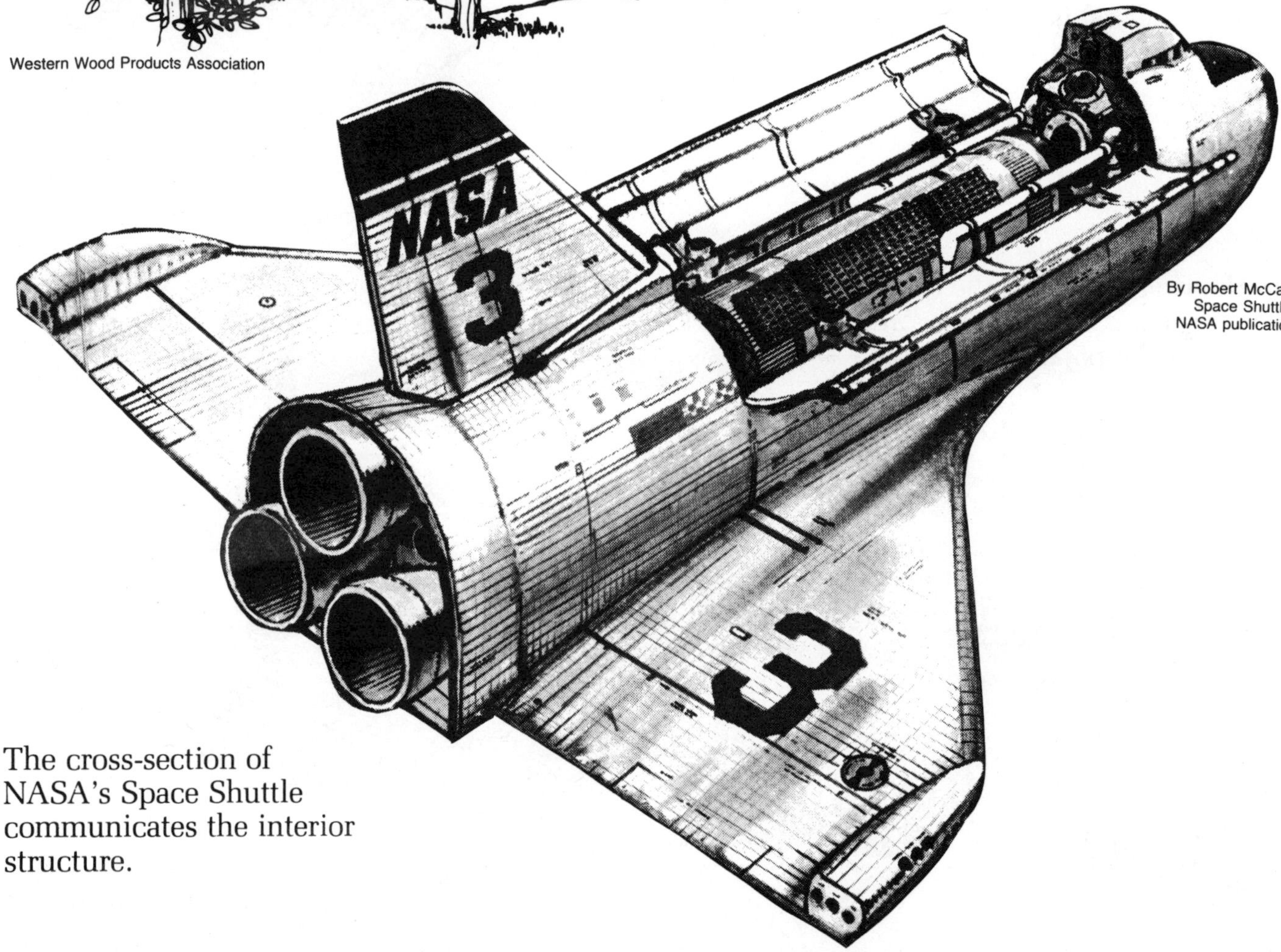

Western Wood Products Association

By Robert McCall,
Space Shuttle,
NASA publication

The cross-section of NASA's Space Shuttle communicates the interior structure.

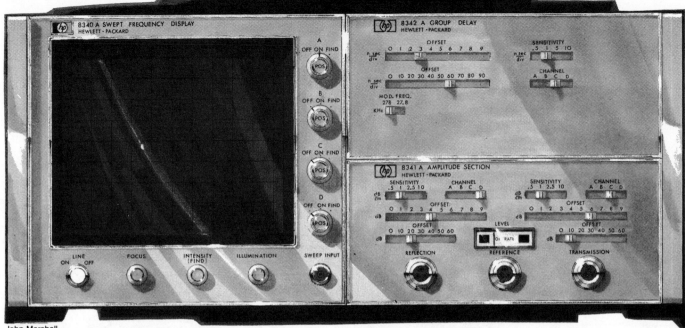

John Marshall

An illustration can give a very real image as shown in the electronic component above.

The line and ink drawing below shows mining as it once was done.

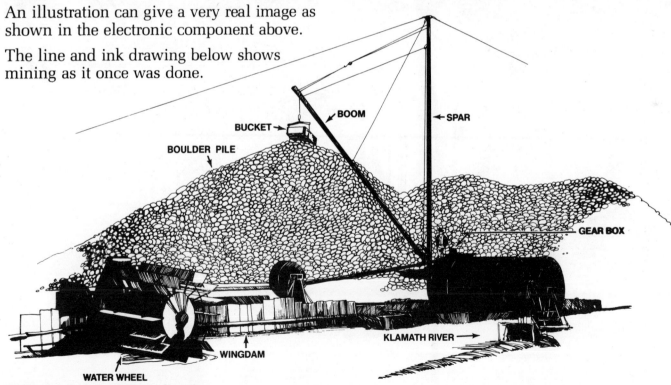

Olinda Hoehne, The Media Mill, Salt Lake City, Utah

221

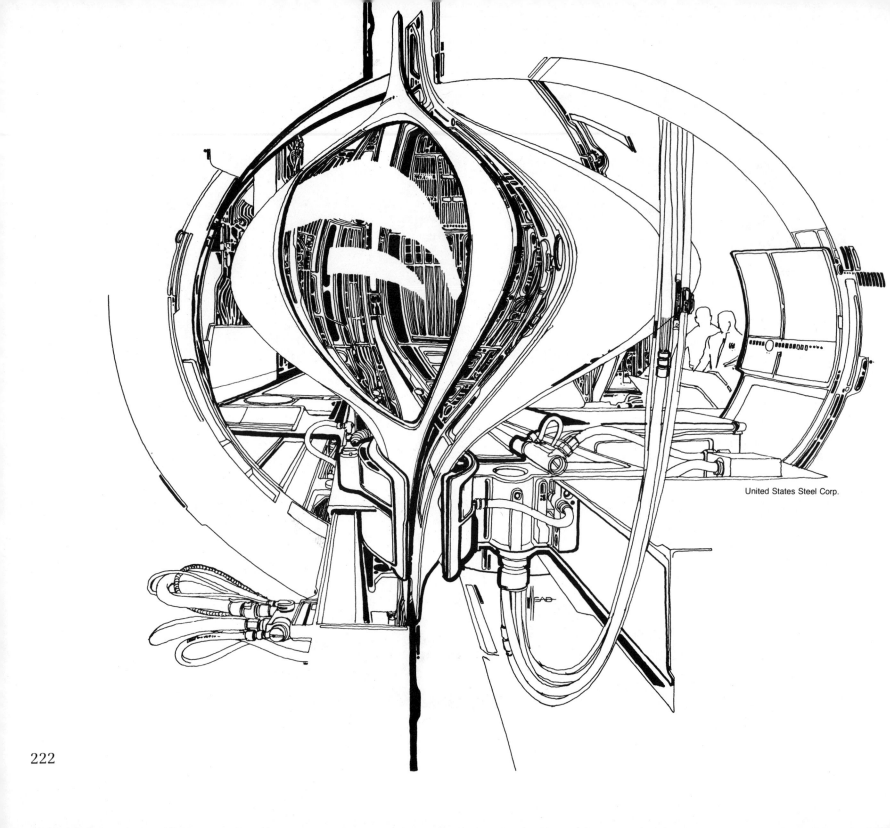

United States Steel Corp.

222

Concept Design Associates, Salt Lake City, Utah

The sequential drawings above show various views of a proposed theme park. This detailed conceptualization helped the developers to "see" what was going to happen. Quite often large building projects need a visual presentation to get them going and built correctly. It helps the developer to be able to visualize what he is spending all those dollars for.

Drawing communicates a proposed shopping center. It gives the feeling of finished reality.

Rodger Zeman

224

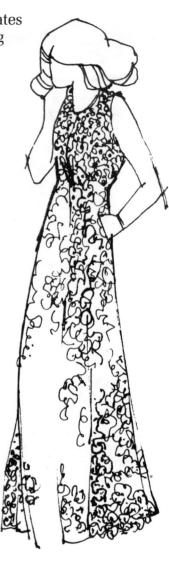

The fashion drawing above helps us buy clothes that we want. Notice especially in this drawing the use of detail to emphasize certain areas. Also notice the feeling of freedom created by leaving out lines such as at the bottom of the dress.

"Drawing is a loose term to which we must accord at least two meanings. It consists first of all, in a perfect comprehension of the structural nature of objects; and secondly in the power of expressing thought and emotion by means of writing down of such structural nature."

Vernon Blake

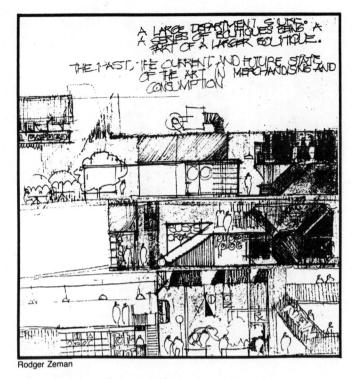

Rodger Zeman

This shows the visualization of a new department store concept.

A cheetah is shown here hunting for food on the African Savanna.

Olinda Hoehne, The Media Mill, Salt Lake City, Utah

A photo reverse of the drawing of a room interior gives a different look to this drawing.

The series of drawings on the right shows a playground area designed for mentally retarded children.

This is a conceptual drawing prepared to help the client visualize proposed communication exhibits. It is of the Champoeg Visitors Center in Oregon.

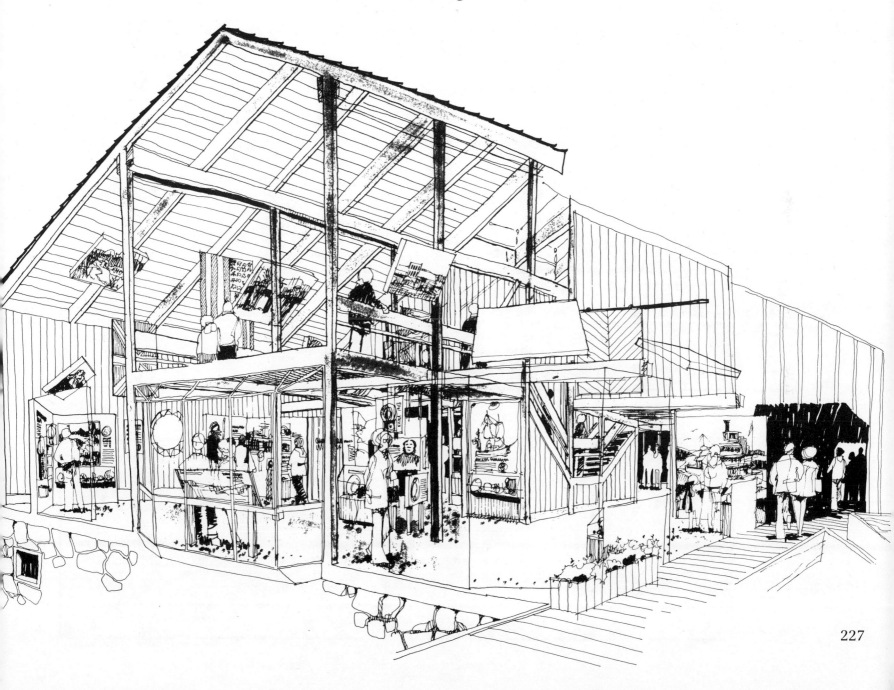

The park, the front view of the automobile and series drawings of a truck hauling pre-fab building materials all were drawn with the intent of visually communicating specific points of interest.

BYU Drawing File

Randy Johnson

228

4-Door Wagon
with optional
simulated woodgrain

4-Door Deluxe Sedan

2-Door Sedan

Sporty SR-5

Ken Dallison, illustrator, Toyota Motor Sales, U.S.A.

Drawings promoting Toyota automobiles
include the action setting for interest and
viewer involvement.

229

230

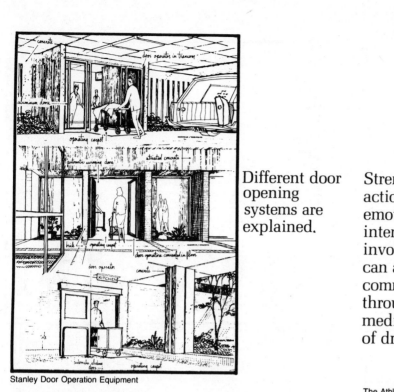

Stanley Door Operation Equipment

Different door opening systems are explained.

Strength, action, emotion, and intense involvement can all be communicated through the medium of drawing.

The illustration at right depicts a home projection unit for big screen video viewing. It includes video and 4-channel sound for a complete experience.

The previous page shows drawings of exhibits built to commemorate the Centennial Year at Brigham Young University in Provo, Utah.

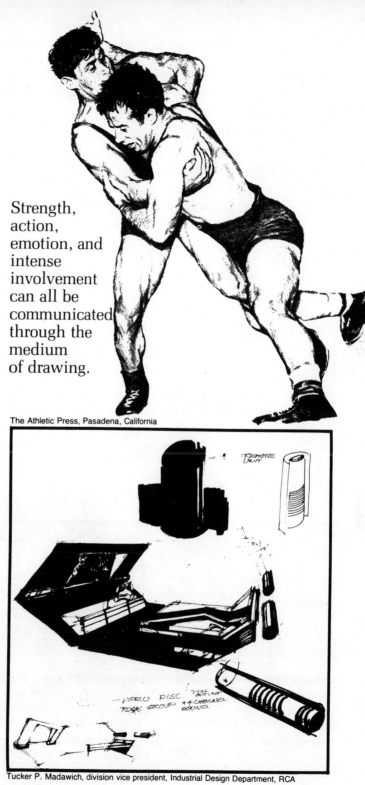

The Athletic Press, Pasadena, California

Tucker P. Madawich, division vice president, Industrial Design Department, RCA

The entrance to a shopping center and a proposed stage setting for a theatrical performance are communicated here through the medium of drawing.

The theatrical set designer roughs out in quick sketch form her stage designs. She places the actors in position, turns the stage lights on and establishes the general visual setting for what is needed in the play. Problems are worked out in advance on paper long before the curtain goes up.

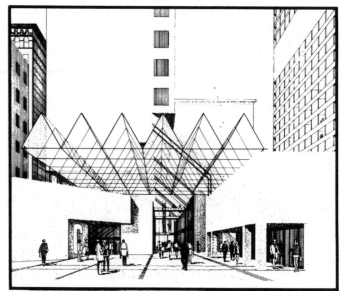

By Ronald Love, First Trust Plaza, Syracuse, Sargent, Webster, Crenshaw & Folley, Syracuse, N.Y.

232

This page employs a loose, free pen and ink drawing to visually portray the entrance to a courtyard.

By Hike Takeda, Community College, Ernest J. KUMP Associates, Palo Alto, California

233

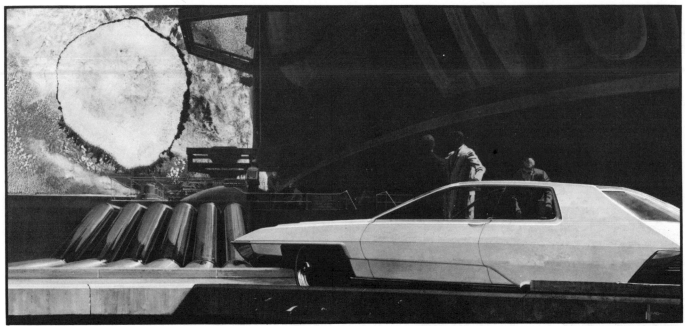

United States Steel Corp.

234

Architects/Planners Alliance, Salt Lake City, Utah

Drawings here show a car of the future, a proposed housing development, the relationship of some internal organs, an open court area of an office building and the power transfer for electric railways.

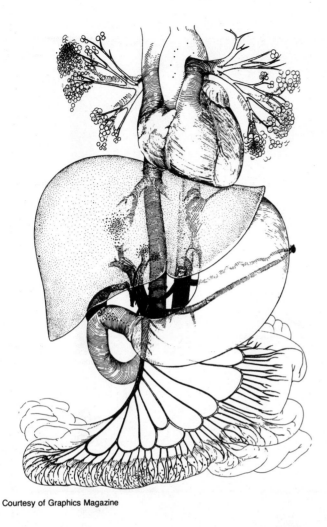

Courtesy of Graphics Magazine

By Jim Hadley, Genessee Hilton Hotel, Warner, Burns, Toan, Lunde Architects, N.Y., N.Y.

"Rail," *Design Magazine*, Richard Draper, ©Design Council, London

235

The End—and the Beginning

We begin life by first noticing the wealth of visual information that surrounds us. Then later we acquire a natural desire to try our hand at expressing what we see and feel about our new world. But as we noted earlier, somewhere along the line many of us become discouraged and quit drawing because of criticism and because our environment places such strong emphasis on verbal expression.

In this book we have attempted to rekindle everyone's natural desire to draw; first, by explaining how our mind works visually in some of the ways we think, and second, by explaining some easy-to-learn visualization and drawing techniques. Drawing can literally "wake up the visual genius," which lies dormant in many of us. Once awakened and developed, this powerful tool can be put to many worthwhile uses.

This is one of the best communicative and viewer involving drawings we have ever found. It was drawn on the floor in an old run down dance studio. People would place their feet over the footprints and learn to dance the fox trot.

Suggested Readings

Through years of work and development, some people become knowledgeable and skilled in particular subjects which have interested them. Often such people have compiled their information into a book, for the convenience and use of others. The following list includes some of the very best books prepared by authors with years of experience in drawing, teaching and developing visualization experiences. Please take time to find and read them all—we are sure you'll find them very helpful.

Drawings as a Means to Architecture, William Kirby Lockard, Van Nostrand Reinhold Co.

Design Drawing and Design Drawing Experiences, William Kirby Lockard, Pepper Publishing

Perspective—A New System for Designers, Jay Doblin, Whitney Library of Design

Graphic Problem-solving for Architects and Builders, Paul Laseau, Cahners Books

Design with Nature, Ian L. McHarg, Doubleday Natural History Press

Pencil Broadsides, Theodore Kautzky, Van Nostrand Reinhold Publishing Corp.

Experiences in Visual Thinking, Robert H. McKim, Brooks/Cole Publishing Co.

The Natural Way to Draw, Kimon Nicolaides, Houghton Mifflin Co.

Perspective Drawing Handbook, Joseph D'Amelio, Tudor Publishing

Architectural Rendering, Albert O. Halse, F.W. Dodge Corp.

Rendering with Pen and Ink, Robert W. Gill, Van Nostrand Reinhold

Mad Magazine, E.C. Publications, Inc.

Visual Thinking, Rudolf Arnheim, University of California Press

Graphic Design for the Computer age, Edward A. Hamilton, Van Nostrand Reinhold

Our World on Space, Robert McCall, Isaac Asimov, New York Graphic Society, Ltd.

Designers Dictionary, Bruce T. Barker, Tony Ken. The Upson Co.

The Pencil, Paul Calle, Watson-Guptill Publications

Language of Drawing, Edward Hill, Prentice-Hall

The Big Yellow Drawing Book, Dan O'Neill, Hugh O'Neill and Associates

Innovations, United State Steel Corporation

Archigram, Peter Cook, Praeger Publishing

Drawing the Head and Figure and *How to Draw Animals*, Jack Hamm, Grosset & Dunlop

Architectural Delineation, Ernest Burden, McGraw Hill

Index

About the Authors

KURT HANKS
works as a design consultant designing primarily Information Centers, Museums and Visitor Centers. He teaches at Brigham Young University in the Department of Art and Design in the Industrial Design Program.

LARRY BELLISTON
is president of an information design firm in Salt Lake City, Utah. He has worked in advertising and public relations with his principal activities centering around graphic arts and mass media communication.